With the Red Wings in the finals, their fans went Cup Crazy – and started seeing things. The Spirit of Detroit donned a Red Wings sweater and a goalie's mask and pads, and a pair of octo-heads showed up at Joe Louis Arena to watch Game 2 on the big screen. The bronze statue got his garb courtesy of Free Press photo technician/illustrator Christine Mackey. Chuck Mallard, left, and Eric Krpichak, both of Garden City, made their cephalopod headgear from papier-mache.

BLOOMFIELD TOWNSHIP PUBLIC LIBRARY
1099 Lone Pine Road
Bloomfield Hills, Michigan 48302-2410

Credits

- **Editors:** Steve Schrader, Bob Ellis
- **Designers:** Bob Ellis, Brian James
- **Photo editors:** Robert St. John, Todd Winge
- **Technology:** Dave Nelson
- **Photo technician:** Christine Mackey
- **Copy editors:** Scott Albert, Brad Betker, Bill Collison, Reid Creager, Owen Davis, Matt Fiorito, Ken Kraemer, Tim Marcinkoski, Karen Park, Shelly Solon
- **Project coordinator:** Dave Robinson
- **Sports editor:** Gene Myers
- **Special thanks:** Laurie Bennett, Bernie Czarniecki, Laurie Delves, Ed Duffy, Linda Erlich, Craig Erlich, Jennifer George, A. J. Hartley, Ed Haun, Wayne Kamidoi, John Lowe, Robert G. McGruder, Tom Panzenhagen, Marcia Prouse, Bill L. Roose, Drew Sharp, Lisa Transiskus
- **Front cover:** Nico Toutenhoofd
- **Front cover design:** Martha Thierry
- **Back cover:** Julian H. Gonzalez

*Dedicated to the memory
of hockey fan and friend
Corky Meinecke*

Detroit Free Press Inc. 1997
321 W. Lafayette Blvd.
Detroit, Mich. 48226

All rights reserved. No part of this book may be reproduced or transmitted in any form or by any means, electronic or mechanical, including photocopying, recording or by an information storage system, without permission of the publisher, except where permitted by law.

To subscribe to the Free Press, call 1-800-395-3300.
Find the Freep on the World Wide Web at www.freep.com

ISBN 0-937247-70-7

A chance to carry the Cup was enough for Scotty Bowman to lace up the skates. Above, Darren McCarty, Martin Lapointe and Mathieu Dandenault celebrate.

Table of contents

Healed by the Cup

42 years of suffering end in one magic night

The crowd was thinning and the noise was dying down. The champagne showers had turned his hair into a sticky nest. Steve Yzerman glanced over the messy remains of the Red Wings' locker room, then told a story.

MITCH ALBOM

He had been in Las Vegas a few years back. He was sitting at a craps table. Two guys from Windsor recognized him and made the typical fuss. *Hey, it's Yzerman from the Red Wings!* Then they looked at the gambling action, looked at The Captain, and one of them whispered, "We better get away from here. There's no luck at this table."

Yzerman "wanted to slug 'em," he recalled.

He didn't, of course. He suffered silently, which is how we do it around Detroit, and the sting of that insult and all the others like it bore deep inside his stomach, churned around like a sleepless wasp, year after year — until one night in June 1997. Until that moment when the final horn sounded and Yzerman threw his stick into the crowd and his curses to the wind and he lifted off toward the open arms of goalie Mike Vernon as a thundering roar shook Joe Louis Arena and you know what? The heck with those guys from Windsor — the whole *world* wanted to be around Steve Yzerman now.

A wounded deer leaps the highest, that's what they say. And if the Red Wings' soaring championship had one common theme it was this: Heal the wounds, mend the tear, end the suffering and leap into salvation. This was not a championship in a city, it was a championship *for* a city, a

Then and now: The Free Press banners the Red Wings' two most recent Stanley Cup titles, 1955 and '97.

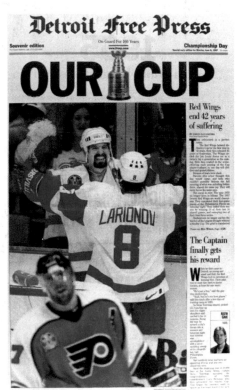

city that has waited 42 years for hockey recognition and is still waiting, thank you, for the non-hockey kind. I got phone calls from radio stations around the country, and they wanted to know whether we burned anything down, if we turned over any police cars, why this was such a big deal. This is the answer I want to give them: "Shut up and get lost. You don't get it and you never will."

But Detroiters will. From the players to the coaches to the season-ticket holders to the kids who stood on street corners waving signs that read, "Honk if you love the Wings!"

This is a story of retribution. Nearly everyone brought some sort of long wait, personal scar or sad history into the Stanley Cup playoffs.

And, as if filled with healing waters, the Cup made them all better.

There was of course, Yzerman, the 32-year-old captain, who has been working down by the Detroit River since Ronald

Reagan's first term. He finally admitted in an emotional moment hours after the Wings won the Cup by beating Philadelphia, 2-1, that the whispers all these years had stung him, even if he never showed it.

"They always say, 'He's a good player but he didn't win it,' " Yzerman said. "And now they can't say that anymore. No matter what, they can't say it, you know? These past five years, there were summers where I didn't even want to go outside, I didn't want to be recognized, I put on my hat, my sunglasses, I walked around in a shell. You're embarrassed. I've felt that way before."

He flicked a champagne drop off his nose. No more embarrassment.

Healed by the Cup.

And how about the two Russian players Yzerman handed that magic trophy off to as the crowd stomped and cheered to "We Are The Champions"? Igor Larionov and Slava Fetisov? Did you see them skating side by side, a 36-year-

BLOOMFIELD TOWNSHIP PUBLIC LIBRARY
1099 Lone Pine Road
Bloomfield Hills, Michigan 48302-2410

old and a 39-year-old, carrying the Cup together, one-handed, the way old women in Europe carry a suitcase? Between these two, they have skated more miles than most starting lineups in the NHL. And yet they always had to hear how Russian players don't want the Cup enough.

"I think we stop that rumor forever now," Larionov said, spilling champagne on whoever passed him in the Wings' locker room. Appreciate it? Both he and Fetisov paid enormous prices to come to North America and make a run at this crown. Fetisov, a major in the Russian Army, was kicked off his team and put behind a desk for speaking up for the right to play in this country. And Larionov had to quit the NHL for a year because the half of his paycheck that was being taken by Mother Russia — supposedly to fund youth sport programs — was instead going toward cell phones for Soviet bureaucrats. Furious, he did the only thing he could do; he cut off their money supply by cutting off his own.

You think he hasn't paid a price to win this Cup?

Or how about the guy to whom the Russians handed off? The Mother of All Facial Hair Growers — Brendan Shanahan? He began the year in Hartford, wondering whether his career was destined to end in oblivion. And there he was kissing the Cup like a long-lost friend.

"Does it match your dream of what it would be like?" I asked Shanahan hours later, as he dashed behind a curtain for another photo with the trophy.

"Match it? It exceeds it!" he gushed. "I want to do it again!"

Healed by the Cup.

There was a sacrifice behind every set of hands that held that chalice and skated around the Joe Louis ice. There was Vernon, ready to sell his house a few months ago because he knew he was about to be traded, and now here he was, the Conn Smythe Trophy winner, the most valuable player in the playoffs.

There was Sergei Fedorov, who swallowed his late-season demotion to defenseman and dug inside himself, discovering his own way back to the star he was supposed to be.

There was Joe Kocur, who was out of hockey altogether, his knuckles a bruised mess. Heck, he was playing in the *recreational leagues* less than six months ago. "The lowest moment," he admitted,

"was when a guy came on the radio and said, the rumor isn't true, Detroit wasn't going to sign me. I heard that and thought, 'That's it. It's over.'"

But here he was holding a cigar. It's never over, as long as you dream.

Healed by the Cup.

There was Kirk Maltby, who once thought his career would be spent in the basement with Edmonton, and Darren McCarty, who fought through personal problems to become the gritty core of this team. When he scored the winning goal against the Flyers — on a dipsy-doodle move that was so unlike him, it had to be heaven-sent — the Wings on the bench jumped so high I thought someone juiced 1,000 volts through their rear ends.

And how about McCarty's best buddy, Kris Draper? Last year at this time, his face was swollen and his jaw was wired shut and he was drinking soup and milkshakes, because Claude Lemieux cheapshotted him in the final game of the failed Western Conference finals. More than any single moment, that blow created a purpose for this year's team.

And more than any single moment, the vengeful beating of Lemieux on March 26 convinced this team that no opponent could contain its spirit.

Now here was Draper, one year after the incident, cigar in teeth, jaw intact, nothing on his chin but the bushy red goatee.

"I don't even remember last June anymore," he boasted.

Healed by the Cup.

The list of soothed scars goes from one end of the roster to the other. But this championship brought salvation for men without numbers, too. There was Scotty Bowman, who heard the critics whisper that he had lost his coaching touch, that 63 was too old to get it done in the NHL anymore. But when he put on skates and did a little lap with the Cup, his players burst into laughter, and a warmth that had never existed between him and his soldiers was suddenly born.

"You know," he said, surveying his team, "when Mr. Ilitch hired me, I told him two years. It's been four."

Will he make it five?

"Ask me in two weeks," he said, but he was smiling, and you wonder if this Cup can't make you younger as well.

And, of course, there was Mike Ilitch himself, who has sunk several fortunes

into his hometown's sports and has watched with clenched fists and a pounding heartbeat year after year, as his teams fell short. He never interfered with players. He never tried to push his businessman's ego into it, believing he could do it better himself — a la George Steinbrenner. And finally, finally, his patience and his dollars were rewarded. "This is the No. 1 thrill," he said, "when Stevie gave me that Cup, and I held it up …"

It looked as if he was going to cry. If he wasn't crying already.

Healed by the Cup.

Now, maybe outsiders read this and think, "What sentimental drivel." Well, that's why they're outsiders. They don't understand what hockey means to this town — more importantly, what pride and camaraderie and unity of spirit mean to this town. We don't get enough. Sometimes economics and urban problems don't let us.

And so, when we get something like a hockey champion — after 42 years of waiting — and when we get a night of peaceful celebration, when we get a night when black and white see no differences between them, only the similarity that one of our own has hit the jackpot — when we get a night like that, we want to squeeze every last star out of its sky. We want the healing power that feeling good can bring.

And if you can't understand that, then go on back to whatever miserable, cynical rock you live under and have a nice day.

"We've had some disappointments and we've broken people's hearts," Yzerman said, "but everybody kept coming back. They kept coming back, every year, and cheering louder."

Strike up the band. No more whispers at the crap table, no more watching Gretzky or Messier with envy. No more Claude Lemieux, no more Patrick Roy, no more ghosts of San Jose, Toronto, St. Louis or anybody else. It's Detroit, now. Detroit. There's a giant 25-foot chalice on our City-County Building, there's a parade, and there's a snapshot in my mind, your mind, and the mind of the man, woman or child sitting next to you as you read this. It's the snapshot of Yzerman and his long-awaited smile, hoisting that trophy high into goosebump land. It pulls us together, that snapshot, and better yet, it always will. They shoot, we soar. Silver threads and golden needles could not mend more than this Cup.

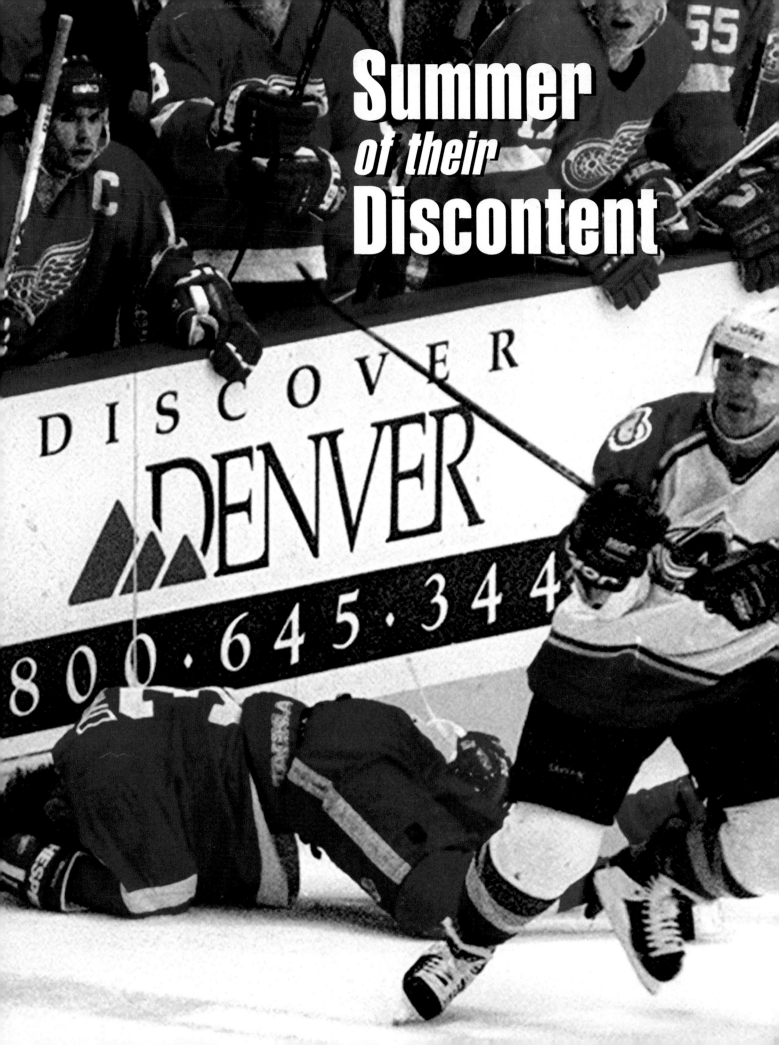

Summer
of their
Discontent

All that remained was the pain

Enduring Colorado fans' taunts both oral and written, Steve Yzerman hangs his head during the final moments
of the Red Wings' 4-1 loss to the Avalanche in Game 6 of the Western Conference finals.
Goalie Mike Vernon, left, right wing Martin Lapointe and trainer John Wharton share the captain's pain.

Playoff fiasco nullifies greatest regular season

Last summer began as most did for the Red Wings: with another painful playoff loss. But this one was more painful than most, as they failed to win a Stanley Cup for the 41st straight year.

By Viv Bernstein and Keith Gave

Another season was over. Another dream dead and buried, this time by an Avalanche. The 1995-96 Red Wings, arguably the greatest team in regular-season history, proved once again they were just that: a great regular-season team.

Not a great playoff team.

Not a champion.

It ended May 29, 1996, at McNichols Arena with a 4-1 loss to Colorado in Game 6 of the Western Conference finals. It ended with a three-goal outburst by the Avalanche in the second period that sent the Wings into summer, sent defenseman Mike Ramsey into retirement without a Stanley Cup, sent fans reeling.

"The expectations of our team, and our own expectation was to get back to the Stanley Cup finals and win, and we didn't do that," captain Steve Yzerman said. "We didn't live up to expectations. We didn't play as well as the Detroit Red Wings are expected to play, as well as we expected to play."

The expectations were even greater this time because of the Wings' season, when they won 62 games, breaking the NHL record of 60 set by Scotty Bowman's 1976-77 Montreal Canadiens (who also won the Cup).

The Wings ran away from the field with their second-straight Presidents' Trophy as the NHL's regular-season champions. To their fans — who sang "I Want Stanley" and threw scores of octopi — another playoff failure was simply unthinkable.

"Obviously, there's a big difference between playoff hockey and regular-season hockey," Yzerman said. "We said it, and we meant it when we said it, winning 62 games during the regular season means nothing. It's not an

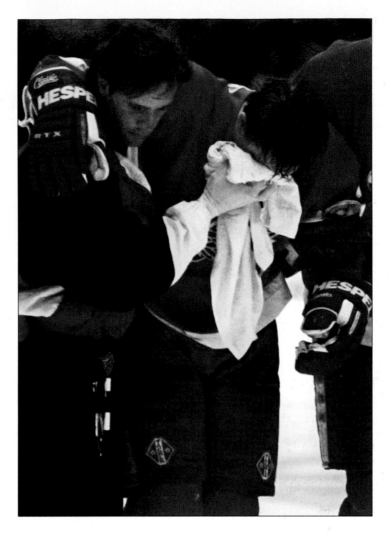

His face smashed like a bowl of eggs, Kris Draper is helped off the ice by trainer John Wharton. The vicious hit by Claude Lemieux broke Draper's jaw and nose, displaced several teeth and gave him a concussion. After the game, still bleeding into a towel, Draper vowed: "I'll be back.'

indicator of what's going to happen in the playoffs. Come playoff time, we didn't respond."

Maybe next season.

For Yzerman.

For Chris Osgood, who established himself as the No. 1 goalie but gave up four goals on 22 shots in the finale.

For Sergei Fedorov and the rest.

Asked why the Wings lost, Bowman said, "They had a player like Joe Sakic. We were banged up a lot and we weren't 100 percent. But we lost to a good team. They were neck-and-neck with us for two years in the league."

The Wings also were hurt by the long road they took to get to the conference finals, including a seven-game series with St. Louis in the semifinals. They didn't have enough gas left for the bigger, more physical Avs, who got big efforts from stars Sakic, Peter Forsberg and Patrick Roy.

"We … were stretched by St. Louis in the previous series, and we never had

time to catch our breath," Bowman said. "We got stronger as the series went on, but we had a lot of elements going against us."

This time, the insult of another playoff loss was made even more bitter by an injury in the first period of the deciding game.

Colorado's Claude Lemieux hit Kris Draper from behind and slammed him into the boards. Draper suffered a broken jaw and nose, a concussion and several displaced teeth; he needed 30 stitches in his mouth and also was cut around his nose and right eye.

Lemieux was assessed a five-minute penalty and ejected, but he returned for the postgame handshakes.

"I can't believe I shook his bleeping hand," Dino Ciccarelli said. "I hadn't seen Kris' face. It's BS. Kris was one of our best players, and Lemieux blindsided him. The poor kid was right by the door, he had his back to him, he didn't have a chance. He was at his mercy. Lemieux could have broken his neck. Hey, they beat us, they had the better team — but that's just BS.

"I probably would have speared him in the face."

There was only one thing the Wings could do for Draper, Osgood said: "We tried to go out there and win the game for him."

They didn't.

Game, series, season.

When Ramsey walked off the ice for what he thought was the last time in his playing career, he had tears in his eyes.

"This is what we do for a living," Darren McCarty said when it was over. "This is our passion. We got our heart torn out."

■ ■ ■

Unfinished business? The Wings had a score to settle with Lemieux, who ended up being suspended for the first two games of the Avalanche's sweep of the Florida Panthers in the finals.

"It makes me sick," said Osgood, Draper's best friend and then his roommate. "He has done it too many times, and I'll say it now: A suspension is not good enough for him anymore.

"He did something we're not going to forget. None of the players are going to forget it.

"When he comes back to play the Red Wings next year, we'll be waiting for him. And he'd better be ready. He can say what he wants about going to the finals. We know we're not going. We can deal with our situation.

"He'd better be ready to deal with what he's going to have to face next season. It's not a threat. It's just something that's going to happen."

Even though Draper's face and heart were broken, he walked out of the arena with a smile and a promise.

"It's not a good way to go out," he said, wiping blood from his mouth with a white towel. "This is a hockey game. I'm out there playing. It's a do-or-die game and I'm doing my best, like everybody else out there, and look at me. Look at my face.

"All of a sudden, I'm there laying on a table getting fixed by four doctors. It's too bad. It's such a great game. It doesn't need this. … It shows absolutely no class.

"I'll see him again. I'll be back, no doubt."

Then he walked out. Smiling.

Avalanche players form a triumphant scrum around goalie Patrick Roy after their series-clinching victory in Game 6. They went on to sweep the Florida Panthers in the Stanley Cup finals.

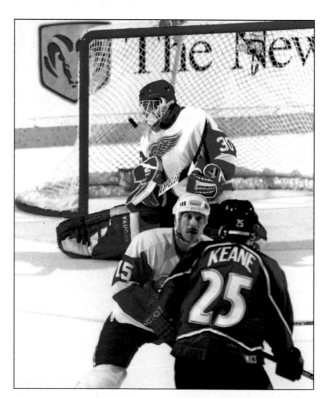

Colorado's Mike Keane watches his shot pass over the shoulder of goalie Chris Osgood, giving the Avalanche a 3-2 victory in Game 1 of the 1996 Western Conference finals. Red Wing Mike Ramsey arrives too late to stop it. Detroit's Paul Coffey put the biscuit in the basket three times in the game – twice for the Red Wings and once, inadvertently, for the Avalanche.

Unwelcome wagon

Keith Primeau refused to report to the Red Wings' camp and skated with the Detroit Whalers.

By Steve Schrader

Call it the summer of our malcontent. Keith Primeau didn't feel welcome in Detroit anymore. He thought he was shouldering too much blame for another Red Wings playoff failure, this time against the Colorado Avalanche.

"It seems as though I'm not wanted there by so many people," Primeau said during Team Canada's World Cup of

Dino's gone, and the Big Kid's going

Hockey training camp.

"I've got a home in Detroit; I've said for several years now that we call Detroit home. That's the worst part about the whole situation, that I still want to be there and I'm not wanted.

"I hate to tab the fans as the culprit. I look at it more as a media thing. People are going to believe what they read in the papers, and every time I turn around, somebody from the media is tearing a strip off of me.

"I've done nothing but extend myself whenever I'm asked. That didn't seem to matter when it came time to find a scapegoat or find somebody they were going to put a negative spin on."

At training camp, which opened in early September without the World Cup contingent, coach Scotty Bowman said the Wings would shop for a trade at Primeau's request.

"He just asked us to explore the opportunity to go somewhere else," Bowman said. "But we're not going to trade a player unless we get a benefit as well. We'll make attempts, but no promises."

After the World Cup, Primeau — who also was unhappy about contract negotiations — made it official Sept. 23: He refused to report to the Wings' training camp. The Wings suspended him; after six seasons, the Big Kid's Red Wings career was over.

And the trade rumors continued to fly.

The early favorite: High-scoring power forward Brendan Shanahan, who had demanded a trade from Hartford.

Here's how some other Wings spent the summer of '96:

■ Kris Draper spent 16 days with his jaw wired shut after it was broken May 29 by Claude Lemieux. Draper lived on milk shakes for breakfast, lunch and dinner.

"I don't think I'll ever have them again," Draper said. "I was mixing all kinds of fruit together, and it tasted OK. But I'd have my fifth one that day and then Ozzie would come home and he'd look all happy because he just had a big steak dinner."

Draper also had a steady diet of doctor appointments and had to cancel a vacation trip with Chris Osgood, his roommate.

"It was a miserable thing for him to go through," trainer John Wharton said. "He lost about 10 pounds. I had him on Ensure, Sustacal, every high-cal, high-protein, low-fat shake you can think of. Everything but Tang.

"I had him over for the first barbecue after he got his jaw unwired. He punished enough chicken breasts to last me a month."

■ Vladimir Konstantinov can take just about any punishment they dish out in the NHL. But on June 14, he suffered a severed left Achilles tendon while playing tennis with Sergei Fedorov.

Konstantinov underwent surgery two days later and was unable to play for Russia in the World Cup. It also was doubtful he would be ready for the Wings'

Do you know the way to Tampa Bay?
Scotty Bowman gives Dino Ciccarelli a few pointers.

Oct. 5 season opener.

■ Right winger Dino Ciccarelli didn't ask to be traded, but he was — Aug. 28 to Tampa Bay for a conditional pick in the 1997 draft.

Ciccarelli was a fan favorite for four seasons, known for his feisty style in front of the net, but he also had numerous battles with Bowman and Wings management.

Other summer departures included defensemen Mike Ramsey, who retired; Marc Bergevin, who signed with St. Louis as a free agent, and TV announcer Dave Strader, who took a job with ESPN.

■ Wings captain Steve Yzerman, a mere fourth-line center on Team Canada, scored at 10:37 of overtime Sept. 10 for a 4-3 victory over Team USA in Game 1 of the World Cup best-of-three finals.

Four months earlier, his double-

overtime winner in Game 7 against St. Louis sent the Red Wings to the Western Conference finals.

"I'm getting used to it," Yzerman said. "That's a good habit to get into."

Team USA coach Ron Wilson complained about the goal, claiming Rod Brind'Amour was "offside by three feet."

"I disagree," Yzerman said. "It was only a foot offside."

Team USA won the next two games and the World Cup.

■ Sept. 25, 1996. A date that will live in infamy in Hockeytown. The day the octopi died.

Tired of seeing the ice littered with scores of octopi and hundreds of rubber rats as they were in the '96 playoffs, the NHL outlawed such fan displays.

The punishment? A two-minute penalty against the home team.

The Season

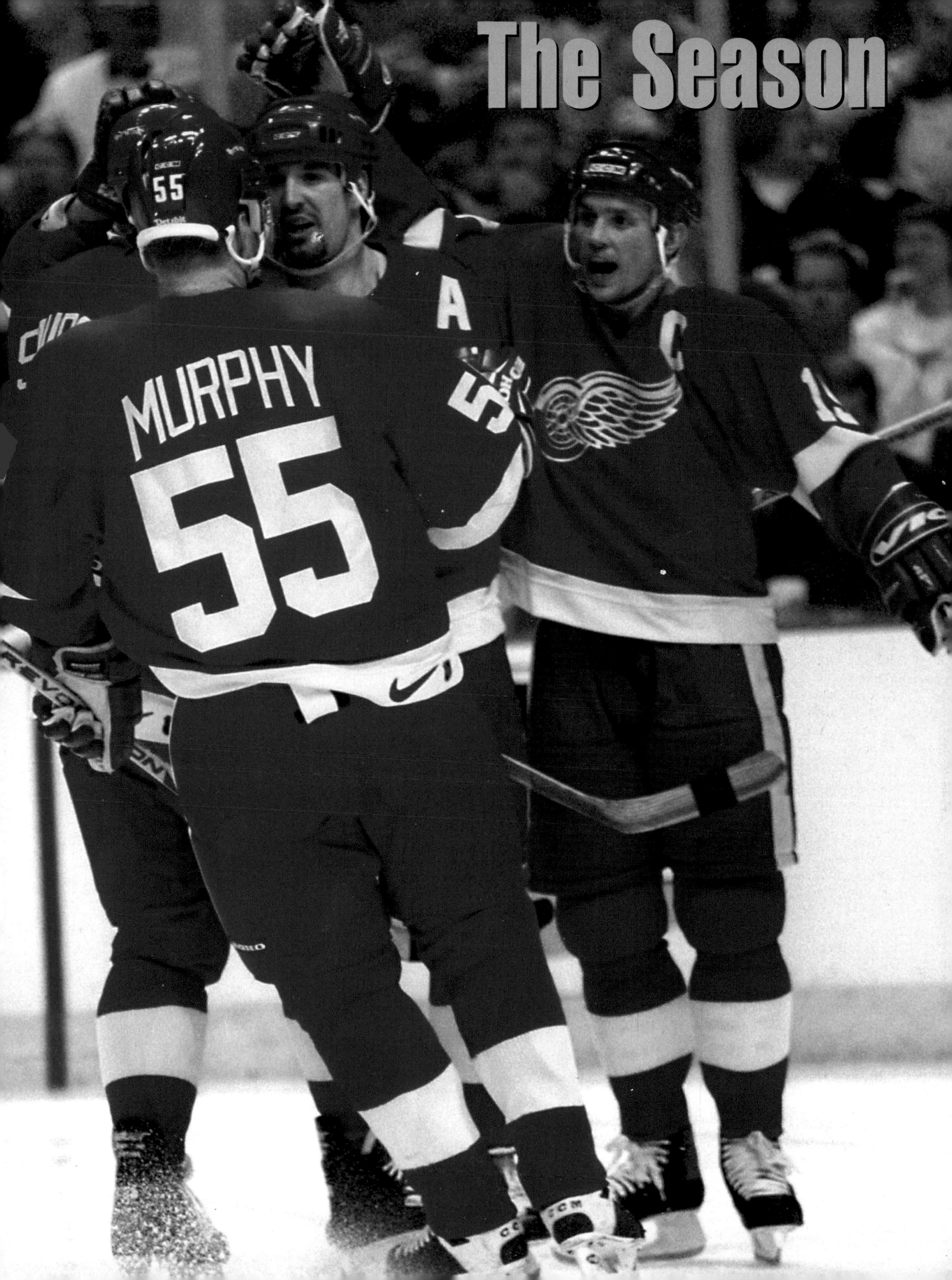

Export of Coffey left Wings gulping

Red Wings players and fans had been teased for weeks about an on-again, off-again trade for Brendan Shanahan. And confusion still reigned two days before the Oct. 9, 1996, home opener.

By Viv Bernstein and Keith Gave

While the Red Wings rallied behind befuddled and emotionally beat-up teammate Paul Coffey, coach Scotty Bowman declared a trade for Hartford's Brendan Shanahan dead again.

"It's too late now," Bowman said. "I don't think it can be resolved. But I was honorable about it. I worked hard at it."

This was Monday. Twice over the weekend, Bowman thought he had a trade. He had proposed sending Keith Primeau, Coffey and a No. 1 draft pick in 1997 to the Whalers for Shanahan, one of the NHL's premier power wingers, and defenseman Brian Glynn.

Rutherford balked Friday on learning Coffey wouldn't report, and again Sunday when he learned Primeau wanted to renegotiate the three-year deal he agreed to Thursday.

On Saturday, Coffey felt he was kicked off the team and sent home from New Jersey before the opener.

But when the weekend came and went without a trade, Coffey phoned neighbor Mike Vernon and said, "Well, I guess I'm going to practice."

After he met for an hour Monday with Bowman, Coffey passed reporters, grinned and said, "That (expletive) 24-hour flu."

But after practice, it was clear the highest-scoring defenseman in NHL history was still reeling.

"It's been tough emotionally," Coffey said. "It's been really tough. Right now I really don't know what's going on. I've

Uncertain deal caused heartburn all around

played out a million different scenarios in my mind the last two days. I'm tired of it. It was just nice to be on the ice with the fellas again."

As for his differences with Bowman, Coffey was content to agree to disagree, strenuously.

"It wasn't like I left the team Saturday, like some people said," Coffey said. "I wasn't going anywhere. There are too many good card games on that plane. I would have stayed for the ride home."

Coffey said he paid for his own flight back to Detroit.

Bowman insisted Coffey could have flown back with the team, adding he kept him out of the game because he wasn't sure how he would play amid the trade talk. He also was worried about Coffey's chronically bad back and didn't want an injury nixing any deal.

Wings captain Steve Yzerman knew what Coffey was enduring. Bowman worked furiously to trade Yzerman to Ottawa just before last season's opener, but the deal fell through.

"Certainly it's unusual," Yzerman said. "I don't really know what to say. Obviously, it's put Coff in a pretty uncomfortable situation, especially for someone of his stature in hockey. …

"It could have been handled differently. I think the more situations like this that occur, the more the gap grows between players and management."

Sergei Fedorov said the turmoil made it difficult to concentrate on hockey in the 3-1 loss to the Devils.

"It did become a distraction for a while," Fedorov said. "That's probably why we couldn't find so much emotion."

We went through a very, very hard week of practice, and we saw some new faces in the locker room before the game. We didn't see old faces like Shawn Burr, Dino Ciccarelli, Mike Ramsey and Marc Bergevin.

"It was quite an adjustment for me. I think it was a learning process. Nobody knows the clear situation. Is anything getting done? Nothing's getting done."

Coffey practiced with the team again Tuesday but still considered his position with the Wings precarious.

"I don't think this thing is over," he said. "I told my wife, don't be getting all excited. You just never know."

■ Yzerman could see some humor in the situation, too.

During a speech at his Tuesday induction into the CATCH Hall of Fame at the Ritz-Carlton in Dearborn, he said Coffey was supposed to be there with him.

But as he and Coffey entered the hotel lobby, he said Bowman jumped out from behind a plant and said: "I'm sorry, Paul, but you can't attend the dinner … and you have to find your own way home."

■ Like Primeau, Shanahan demanded a trade. But he didn't hold out and thus felt the home fans' wrath in the Whalers' opening 1-0 victory over Phoenix.

They booed and chanted, "We want Primeau!"

"It hurt, of course, but I don't think it was anything I didn't expect," Shanahan said. "I understand. I don't think the fans were out of line. They have a right to express themselves. If this was my hometown and somebody had asked for a trade, I'd be upset, too.

"When you look at the broader picture, life's still pretty good. So getting booed and having signs written about you and going through all this, you realize we're still pretty fortunate men to be playing this game."

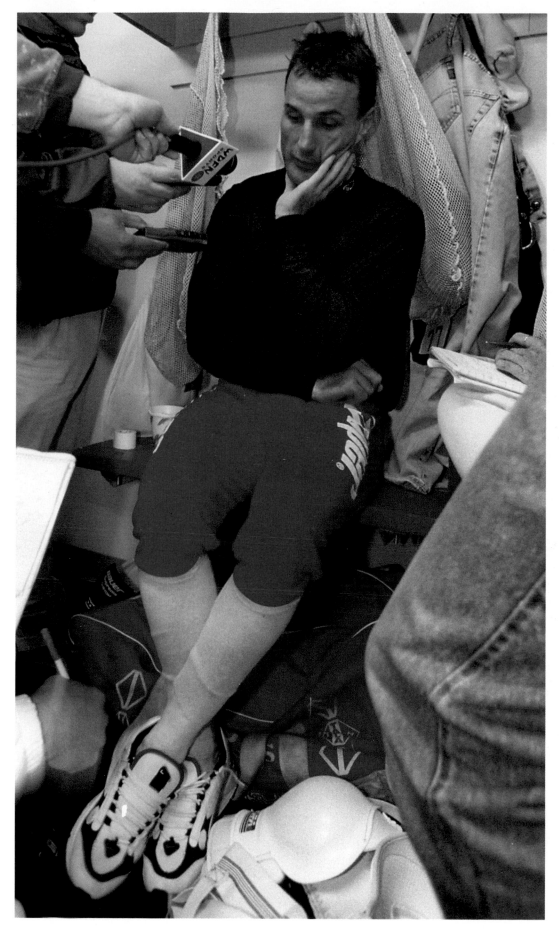

Red Wing Paul Coffey discusses his tentative situation with the Detroit newspaper and broadcast reporters. "It's been tough emotionally," he said. "It's been really tough. Right now I really don't know what's going on. I've played out a million different scenarios in my head the last two days. I'm tired of it." Within days, he was traded to Hartford. He wound up the season with the Philadelphia Flyers.

Welcome to Shannytown

Brendan Shanahan, who made his Wings debut in a hurry, quickly became an instant success with his new teammates and fans.

At the last minute, the Wings finally get the forward they had covetted for so long

The rumor, the on-again, off-again trade, became reality Oct. 9, 1996, when the Red Wings acquired Brendan Shanahan from the Hartford Whalers.

By Mitch Albom

The phone rang around 3:30 Wednesday afternoon. Paul Boyer, the equipment man, picked it up. "Who wears No. 14 for us?" asked Scotty Bowman, the Red Wings coach.

"Aaron Ward," Boyer said.

"Make a new No. 14 with the name 'Shanahan.' Give Ward No. 27. You think he'll mind?"

"No," Boyer said, smiling, "I don't think he'll mind."

This is how Opening Day of hockey in Detroit began: with a phone call, and a new number. Boyer called East Side Sports, where the uniforms are made, and

Shanahan, second from the left, made it in time for introductions for the home opener at Joe Louis Arena. He had arrived only 11 minutes before.

How Brendan Shanahan made it to the Joe on time for the home opener:

■ **NOON**

Mike Ilitch's jet dispatched to Hartford.

■ **1 P.M.**

Trade consummated, sending Shanahan and defenseman Brian Glynn to the Red Wings for Keith Primeau, Paul Coffey and 1997 No. 1 draft pick. The Whalers made the deal even though Primeau had not agreed to terms, nor had Coffey agreed to report.

■ **4:45**

Shanahan flies from Hartford, with instructions to return if any hitch develops.

■ **5:05**

Coffey leaves Joe Louis Arena.

■ **5:15**

Whalers announce deal has been made.

■ **6:05**

Scotty Bowman holds news conference.

■ **6:44**

■ 6:44: Shanahan arrives at Joe Louis Arena wearing a dark blue suit. His equipment, still in a Whalers No. 94 bag, is brought in a minute later by Wings equipment manager Paul Boyer.

■ **6:55**

Shanahan, wearing No. 14, first appears in a Wings uniform in the pregame skate.

■ **7:37**

Players are introduced. Shanahan and Steve Yzerman draw loudest ovations.

■ **7:47**

Shanahan's first shift as a Red Wing, with Yzerman on the right and Sergei Fedorov at center. In the second period of the 2-0 victory, Shanahan cross-checked Edmonton defenseman Greg de Vries. No penalty was called, but Shanahan was suspended for one game and fined $1,000 by the league.

two hours later, it was in his hands. He took a roll of two-sided tape, and stuck a red "A" onto the sweater's chest.

They come and they go. That's a famous line about athletes — and it sure held true Wednesday.

In the morning, Keith Primeau and Paul Coffey were still Red Wings. By the afternoon, they belonged to Hartford, and Brendan Shanahan, 27, the much-coveted forward with the physical reputation, was on team owner Mike Ilitch's plane to center ice in his new home, the Motor City.

Shanahan arrived at Joe Louis Arena at 6:44 p.m. and was on the ice 11 minutes later.

"It's been a pretty hectic day," Shanahan said, after his first night was over and the Wings had defeated Edmonton, 2-0, in their home opener.

"I was really nervous when I got here. But the first thing someone said when I got to the locker room was they were waiting for me, so we could all skate out for warmups as a team. That was nice."

That was just the start. Shanahan was introduced to the crowd, and his very name brought an explosion of noise — "AT FORWARD, NO. 14 BRENDAN SHANAHAN" — and as he skated out, the anticipation had to be burning inside.

Anyone who has been playing in the lifeless Hartford Civic Center would think he had died and gone to heaven waking up in the hysterics of Joe Louis.

MEET SHANNY

WHO: Left wing Brendan Shanahan, one of the NHL's premier power forwards.

PERSONAL: 6-foot-3, 215 pounds … born in Mimico, Ontario … 28 years old.

ROAD TO HOCKEYTOWN: Drafted by New Jersey second overall behind Pierre Turgeon in 1987 (draft was held at Joe Louis Arena) … played four seasons for Devils … signed as free agent with St. Louis in summer of '91 … … played four seasons for Blues, twice scoring 50 goals … traded to Hartford for Chris Pronger in summer of '95 … scored 44 goals in only season with Whalers, then asked to be traded.

THE BIG DEAL: Traded from Hartford to Red Wings on Oct. 9, 1996, with Brian Glynn to the Red Wings for Keith Primeau, Paul Coffey and 1997 No. 1 draft pick.

Brendan Shanahan was the Wings' season leader in goals with 47 and points with 88.

RED WINGS FIRSTS

GAME: Started season with Whalers but trade went through in time for Wings' home opener, Oct. 9 against Edmonton.

POINT: After sitting out one-game suspension for cross-checking, drew assist for 600th career point in second game with Wings, 6-1 victory Oct. 12 at Buffalo.

GOAL: Scored twice Oct. 21 in sixth game as Wing, a 3-0 victory over Los Angeles.

HAT TRICK: Natural hat trick included 300th career goal in 5-2 victory at home over Toronto on Nov. 27.

SEASON HIGHLIGHTS

STAR POWER: Scored power-play goal as Western Conference lost All-Star Game, 11-7, on Jan. 18.

HATS OFF: Scored consecutive hat tricks Feb. 8 and Feb. 12 in 6-5 victory at Pittsburgh (including OT winner) and 7-1 victory over San Jose.

MR. FEBRUARY: NHL player of the month with 14 goals and 21 points in 13 games.

LEADING MAN: Led Wings with 47 goals and 88 points (giving him 335 goals and 686 points for career).

BLARNEY

Various team media guides have listed Shanahan as an accomplished saxophonist, an actor, a pro soccer goalie, a tennis ball boy during an Andre Agassi match at the U.S. Open and a mountain climber.

"That just all started because my summers are too boring to put down in the media guide," he said. "I told a few white lies the first year and after that, I was getting letters from people contributing what they thought would be a good idea. I had to put a stop to it. It was getting out of control."

"I was thrilled," Shanahan admitted.

And just a few minutes later, he was skating up the ice alongside Steve Yzerman and Sergei Fedorov, the "A" on his sweater, stuck on with Boyer's two-sided tape — only in hockey can you be the alternate captain on a team before you even know your teammates' names — and before five minutes had passed, Shanahan was in a fight, and he went to the penalty box.

Hmmm. Feels like he's been here a lifetime.

"Are you ready for the pressure of the expectations?" someone asked Shanahan after the game. "Some people see you as the missing piece of the puzzle."

"Well, I am that … a piece," he said. "But just a piece. I'm not the guy who's going to change things."

Maybe so, maybe no. The Wings expect big noise from this young man, and they gave up a lot to get him. Granted, Primeau didn't want to play in this town anymore, and Coffey is 35, but not so long ago, we mentioned those guys near the top of the Detroit "stars" list. Don't be too quick to discount their value.

Of course, Shanahan brings value as well. A powerful left winger who could score 50 or more goals with an offense like Detroit's, he's a guy who has been waiting all his life for a team like this.

"When I heard the crowd cheering tonight, I looked around, and I felt great," he said. "Compared to the events of the last few days (he was booed in Hartford when he let it be known he wanted out), this was the feeling I wanted.

"The Red Wings' game plan is to win a Stanley Cup, and that's my goal, too. I don't look at this as the end of something, I look at it as the beginning."

That's a good approach. The Wings saw it that way, too. They gave away old, they gave away unhappy, they got young and hungry. Most of the time that works.

Meanwhile, you have to marvel at the quick-changing fortunes of pro sports, where a veteran, in one night, goes from playing hockey to watching baseball, while another guy slaps a sticky-taped "A" on his uniform and gets a standing ovation.

It's the start of a long parade, this hockey season. From the look of it, we'd better buckle up.

COFFEY TALKS

By Viv Bernstein and Helene St. James

Paul Coffey was told he would play in the Red Wings' Oct. 9 home opener against Edmonton. He skated with the team in the morning, went home and returned to Joe Louis Arena for the pregame skate.

"I didn't hear anything," Coffey said. "I just walked down to the dressing room. I saw (assistant equipment manager) Tim Abbott. His face kind of dropped."

That's when Coffey knew he had been traded. The Hartford rumors had come true, though he had received no phone call from Wings coach Scotty Bowman or Whalers general manager Jim Rutherford.

Coffey left without talking to Bowman. "I can't believe I didn't say good-bye to him," he said, his trademark wit still intact.

"I said, 'Just tell him it's fine, I'm out of here.' I don't have anything bad to say about him. It's not worth it. People who have to say bad things about other people are just trying to make themselves look good.

"I have good memories of Detroit. I'm not going to let one week taint my four years here. This is a minor hurdle."

Coffey reluctantly reported to Hartford with Keith Primeau. Enforcer Stu Grimson also soon became a Whaler, claimed on waivers.

The three former Wings returned for a Nov. 4 game, a 5-1 Detroit victory. Only Primeau was booed, but he was used to hearing that at the Joe.

"It was what I expected," Primeau said. "It was par for the course."

"It was one of those games you just want to get it over with," Coffey said. "This isn't my home anymore. The day I got traded, that's it. Life goes on. If you want to sit and worry about it and

make yourself homesick, you're just going to put yourself through torture. You have to get on with your life."

Which for Coffey meant getting out of Hartford, and he eventually was traded to Philadelphia.

While Coffey generally avoided a public war of words with Bowman, other departed Wings weren't shy about tossing darts in the coach's

Neither Paul Coffey nor his fans were happy about his departure.

direction later in the season.

Such as Dino Ciccarelli, who was traded to Tampa Bay in the offseason; Bob Errey, claimed off waivers by San Jose in February; and Shawn Burr, traded to the Lightning after the '95 season.

"He's done some things to people that you just wouldn't believe," Ciccarelli said. "Obviously, as a hockey coach he's the best ever. But as a person? He's a jerk. … But ask anyone who ever played for him and they'll tell you that same thing.

"He's a great coach and a terrible person. And that's that."

A night to remember for Sergei

Sergei Fedorov gave Vladimir Konstantinov a hug after Konstantinov gave him four assists that December night against Washington. Fedorov scored five goals, including the winner in overtime.

Fedorov comes alive for five goals

Thursday, Dec. 26

It certainly wasn't the easiest of seasons for Sergei Fedorov. At times, as he bounced from the top scoring line to checking line to defense, he seemed a mere shadow of the player who once scored 56 goals and won the Hart Trophy as the NHL's most valuable player. His troubles still weren't over, but never did his star shine brighter than on this night.

By Helene St. James

Welcome back, Sergei. Fedorov scored all five goals Thursday, including the winner with 2:21 left in overtime, as the Red Wings beat Washington, 5-4, at Joe Louis Arena.

"This night was like rolling stones from the mountain coming at me," Fedorov said. "I was very excited, because the overtime goal, that's the most exciting part of the game."

It was his first five-goal night, second four-goal performance and third career hat trick.

Fedorov's other four-goal game was Feb. 12, 1995, in a 4-4 tie with Los Angeles. That same night he missed on a penalty shot in overtime.

Only one Wing has ever done better: Syd Howe, who scored six against the Rangers on Feb. 3, 1944.

Fedorov's big night capped an amazing turnaround for him. Of his 17 goals to that point, 12 came in the past 11 games. (He finished with 30, his lowest output for a full season.)

His December resurgence coincided with the reunification of the Russian Five. Even though he now has seven years' experience in North America, Fedorov is at his best when he plays Russian-style hockey.

While Fedorov was scoring five goals, Vladimir Konstantinov was recording four assists, Igor Larionov three and Slava Fetisov one.

"I'm glad for Sergei because he needed confidence," Larionov said. "I don't think it's right for someone of his skills to be somewhere in the shadows. He's a superstar, and he has to be the center of attention. It's a shame for him to be somewhere in the middle."

And that is where Fedorov found himself after scoring one goal in his first 11 games, when coach Scotty Bowman had him on a line with Brendan Shanahan and Steve Yzerman.

"It's easiest for Sergei when we play together," Larionov said. "It's easier for him to fulfill all his quantities. He's a goal-scorer, he's a playmaker, he's a defensive forward. It's easier when you've got somebody right beside him who knows what he's doing.

"In our Russian system, we have different responsibilities," Larionov said. "If you play a five-man unit, everybody should play offense, everybody should play defense. But some guys have more skills to play offense.

"Sergei is like that. He can beat two or three guys by himself. He's got that taste for scoring goals, and I would like him to do that every game. It's a good sign when you've got so much confidence."

And perspective.

"The most important scoring was the fifth goal," Fedorov said. "That's what gives you the win, that's what gets you to the next round, that's what gives you maybe the Stanley Cup."

Five alive

How Sergei Fedorov scored his five goals against Washington:

1 Fired puck high past Jim Carey at 7:32 of first period. **1-0, Wings.**

2 Grabbed loose puck at the red line, skated in alone and beat Carey high again at 3:46 of second, 40 seconds after Peter Bondra scored for the Capitals. **2-1, Wings.**

3 Brendan Shanahan sent a pass between his legs to Vladimir Konstantinov, who fed the puck to Fedorov just outside the crease at 10:33 of the third. **3-3.**

4 Forced overtime at 12:08, just 41 seconds after Dale Hunter had given Caps the lead. **4-4.**

5 Beat Carey again 2:39 into overtime. **5-4, Wings.**

On any other day...

Even with the five-goal game, Fedorov displayed some bad timing. It came on the same day the Lions fired coach Wayne Fontes and was bumped off the front page.

Sagging in the middle

The Wings' bench was not a happy place in January '97. They went 0-3-2 at Joe Louis Arena for the month.

Midseason form a slouch compared to '95-96

By Helene St. James

As a portrait of a Stanley Cup champion, the Red Wings were still a work very much in progress halfway through the season.

They were merely a contender, not the overwhelming favorite they had been in recent seasons.

As the new year started, the Wings seemed to slip even a notch further, starting with a 2-1 loss to Dallas, the first time the Stars had won at Joe Louis Arena in 15 tries.

The loss in Game 39 left them at 20-13-6 on Jan. 3. The previous season, their 13th loss didn't come until Game 76 — and it was their last loss, as they finished 62-13-7 and set an NHL record for victories.

January 1997 would end as it began, with a loss at the Joe. And no home victories in between.

The Wings were 0-3-2 at home in January. They hadn't gone a multiple-home game calendar month without a victory since 1982, when they were 0-3-2

Dallas center Mike Modano gave the Stars a 2-1 victory Jan. 3, their first triumph in 15 tries at the Joe.

in November.

Overall, the Wings had gone 2-6-3 since a three-game winning streak in late December.

Their last chance to break the January Joe jinx was Jan. 29 against Phoenix, but they were shut out, 3-0.

"It was a lousy effort," captain Steve Yzerman said. "We didn't come to play. It

doesn't matter if the team is first overall or in last place. I think we're too cocky, and we have no reason to be cocky."

Brendan Shanahan agreed: "We're all ashamed of ourselves. There are no excuses for coming out and playing the way we did. We should have our heads examined. …

"We're stupid if we think we can throw our sticks on the ice and teams will kneel down and say, 'Here are two points.' "

The Wings weren't looking for excuses, even though Sergei Fedorov missed almost a month because of a groin injury, Chris Osgood was sidelined in mid-January with a sore hamstring, and associate coach Barry Smith was on leave, coaching a team in Sweden.

"You come to the rink some days, and play the game and sit down after the game and say, 'What a rotten game, I didn't show up, I didn't come ready to play, and it's going to change,' " Yzerman said. "Before you know it, five games have gone by.

"Too many games have gone by where we haven't been ready to play. We have to stop right now and really make a conscientious effort to be prepared for practices, for games, and it's solely upon the shoulders of the players."

It was also clear in January that the

The Wings suffered their 13th loss of the season in the Jan. 3 game vs. Dallas. They had lost only 13 the entire previous regular season.

Wings had something else to worry about. Not only was Colorado headed for the Presidents' Trophy for the NHL's best regular-season record, the Wings faced a new challenge in Dallas.

The Wings and Stars seemed to be teams headed in opposite directions.

After finishing last in the Central Division and out of the playoffs the previous season, Dallas started 1996-97 with six straight victories.

The woeful January, including a 6-3 loss at Dallas on Jan. 8, dropped the Wings into third place, nine points behind the Central Division leader and one behind St. Louis.

The Wings wouldn't be able to overcome that deficit to Dallas, but they won the next meeting: 4-3 on Slava Kozlov's overtime goal on Feb. 2 for their first home victory of '97.

Kozlov tipped in Igor Larionov's pass at 1:20 of OT. After a three-game benching, it was his second straight game with a goal and the Wings' first two-game winning streak of the year.

"The goal I got Saturday was like a Christmas present," Kozlov said. "The one from Igor was like a Valentine's Day present."

Scotty Bowman shared a handshake and smile with his players after he set the record for all-time victories on Feb. 8 with 1,000. His regular-season total is now 1,013.

Scotty's magic number: 1,000

Being liked doesn't really matter to Scotty Bowman. All that matters is winning.

Like him or not, Bowman knows how to win

"You hated him for 364 days a year. And on the 365th day, you collected your Stanley Cup rings."
— Steve Shutt, former Montreal Canadien

By Keith Gave and Jason La Canfora

Not all of them hated Scotty Bowman. Every now and then, a guy like Mike Ramsey would see the bullheaded Scotsman for what he is: a man behind the coach with the all-time record for NHL victories.

"There are a lot of times when there's a human being there," said Ramsey, who played for Bowman in Buffalo, Pittsburgh and Detroit.

And whether they liked him never really mattered to Bowman. All that matters i s winning, which is what his teams have done a record 1,013 times in his 25 seasons.

No. 1,000 came Feb. 8 with a 6-5 victory at Pittsburgh. Typically, Bowman wasn't exactly bowled over by his accomplishment.

"It's nice you don't have to think about it anymore," he said. "I mean, when we started the season, I needed 25, I knew that. But I thought I would do it before now."

The last few didn't come easily. Bowman started the 1997 calendar year needing five victories, but the Wings went

Scotty's career

Through the years

Season	Team	W	L	T	Pct.
1967-68	St. Louis	23	21	14	.517
1968-69	St. Louis	37	25	14	.579
1969-70	St. Louis	37	27	12	.566
1970-71	St. Louis	13	10	5	.554
1971-72	Montreal	46	16	16	.692
1972-73	Montreal	52	10	16	.769
1973-74	Montreal	45	24	9	.635
1974-75	Montreal	47	14	19	.706
1975-76	Montreal	58	11	11	.794
1976-77	Montreal	60	8	12	.825
1977-78	Montreal	59	10	11	.806
1978-79	Montreal	52	17	11	.719
1979-80	Buffalo	47	17	16	.688
1981-82	Buffalo	18	10	7	.614
1982-83	Buffalo	38	29	13	.556
1983-84	Buffalo	48	25	7	.644
1984-85	Buffalo	38	28	14	.563
1985-86	Buffalo	18	18	1	.500
1986-87	Buffalo	3	7	2	.385
1991-92	Pittsburgh	39	32	9	.544
1992-93	Pittsburgh	56	21	7	.708
1993-94	Detroit	46	30	8	.595
1995	Detroit	33	11	4	.729
1995-96	Detroit	62	13	7	.799
1996-97	Detroit	38	26	18	.573
Totals		**1,013**	**460**	**263**	**.659**

Everything you wanted to know about Scotty Bowman's remarkable coaching career:

■ Started NHL career in St. Louis in the 1967-68 season. His first 110 victories came with the expansion Blues, whom he took to the Stanley Cup finals three times.

■ Bowman's 200th, 300th, 400th and 500th victories — and five Stanley Cups — came during his eight glorious seasons with Montreal in the '70s. One of those Cups followed a then-record 60-victory regular season in 1976-77.

■ Left the Canadiens and added general manager tittle in Buffalo, where he gained his 600th and 700th victories.

■ After four seasons away from coaching, Bowman had a successful, two-year stint in Pittsburgh when the late Bob Johnson became ill. He got his 800th victory and, in 1992, his sixth Stanley Cup with the Penguins.

■ Bowman is 179-80-37 (.667) in four seasons with the Wings, pushing his victory total to 1,013. Al Arbour is second with 781, and only three men have won more games with the Wings: Jack Adams, 413; Sid Abel, 340; and Tommy Ivan, 262. Bowman was named coach of the year after the record-breaking 62 victories in 1995-96 (he also won the award in '77). And, of course, he won his

Scotty Bowman simply shrugs off all the attention given to his career milestones.

seventh Stanley Cup as a coach.

■ He has coached 1,736 games against 34 teams, including defunct franchises and teams that played in multiple locations. And he has a winning record against all of them.

■ Has coached the most games against Los Angeles, with 113. He has also beaten the Kings and Pittsburgh the most, with 65 victories, followed by Minnesota/Dallas at 64.

■ Best winning percentage is against Washington, 56-8-5 for .848. He was 47-21-16 (.655) coaching against Wings.

■ Has lost most often to Boston, with 40 defeats in 108 games.

---

into a 2-5-3 tailspin.

Victories over St. Louis and Dallas put him at 999 and counting. The Wings had two chances to give Bowman No. 1,000 at home, but tied St. Louis and lost to Vancouver.

Then the big victory came at Pittsburgh, when Brendan Shanahan completed his hat trick in overtime.

Tear another page out of the record book, and hand it to Scotty Bowman.

"Nobody, at least in my lifetime and the next couple of generations, is going to come close to Scotty as far as the wins go," said Los Angeles Kings coach Larry Robinson, who played for Bowman during the Montreal dynasty of the 1970s. "I don't know anybody who can last that long anymore. I'm in my second year, and it takes its toll."

Consider that Bowman has averaged 40 victories, including four partial seasons. Any coach will say 40 is a benchmark for a

very good season. Bowman's teams have surpassed 50 victories seven times. Twice his teams have reached 60, including last season's NHL-record 62 with the Wings.

"In coaching a full season, he's never had a losing record," said Stars coach Ken Hitchcock. "That's absolutely remarkable. He's the master of accountability and responsibility.

"To me, he's like Bobby Knight. It doesn't matter how big a star you are on his team, you're accountable. When his team's not playing well, he leaves them alone. When the team is going good, he's all over them."

Many around him suggest Bowman's style borders on tyranny, though some say he has managed to adapt to changing times.

"I think he's changed a little, but not a lot," said Brian Engblom, an ESPN

broadcaster who played for Bowman in Montreal. "He always controlled the environment completely.

"He knew exactly what was going on all the time. It amazed me. He knew everything about the referees and other things I had never thought of. He was on top of everything."

Because his 1,000th victory occurred on the road, the Wings saluted Bowman's achievement at Joe Louis Arena on March 19, before a 4-1 victory over Boston (No. 1,009).

Bowman's brother Jack was there for the occasion, but merely by chance. He was scouting for the Buffalo Sabres.

"I called Scotty this morning and said I might come to Detroit," Jack Bowman said, "and he never even mentioned the ceremony. Maybe when it's all said and done, he'll appreciate what this accomplishment means."

One in a thousand

Captain Steve Yzerman stands alone, a symbol of Red Wings hockey since 1983.

Yzerman joins greats Howe, Delvecchio

Wednesday, Feb. 19, 1997

Sometimes it seems Steve Yzerman, 32, has been a Red Wing forever. He began wearing the Winged Wheel as an 18-year-old and this season played in his 1,000th game as a Wing.

By Helene St. James and Keith Gave

Another year, another milestone for Red Wings captain Steve Yzerman. And he celebrated his 1,000 game as a Wing by assisting on three of their four goals Wednesday night in a 4-0 shutout of Calgary at Joe Louis Arena.

Yzerman, the Wings' first choice, fourth overall, in the 1983 draft, played his first NHL game Oct. 5, 1983, at Winnipeg, where he scored a goal and an assist. After 14 seasons, he has 539 goals, 801 assists and 1,340 points.

"It's a neat thing to do," Yzerman said after joining Gordie Howe and Alex Delvecchio as Red Wings with 1,000 regular-season games.

"I don't know how many guys have done it all with one team.

"It gives you a chance to reflect on different situations that you've been in. I've played with a lot of guys and been through a lot here. It's all been in Detroit, but I feel like I've been on four or five

Says team owner Mike Ilitch: "Steve Yzerman really wants to win, and he exemplifies that with his heart."

BIG NUMBERS

Here's how Steve Yzerman ranks with all-time Red Wings greats (Detroit statistics only):

SCORING	G	A	PTS
Gordie Howe	786	1,023	1,809
Steve Yzerman	539	801	1,340
Alex Delvecchio	456	825	1,281
Norm Ullman	324	434	758
Ted Lindsay	335	393	728
Sergei Fedorov	242	350	592

SERVICE	YRS	GP
Gordie Howe	25	1,687
Alex Delvecchio	24	1,549
Steve Yzerman	14	1,023
Marcel Pronovost	15	983
Norm Ullman	13	875

BIG NIGHTS

The major milestones of Yzerman's career:

■ Feb. 24, 1993: Assisted on a Keith Primeau goal during a 10-7 loss at Buffalo for his 1,000th career point.

■ Jan. 17, 1996: Scored 500th career goal against Colorado's Patrick Roy in a 3-2 victory at home last season. To celebrate, he took his family to Disney World (it was All-Star weekend, and he wasn't invited).

■ Nov. 21, 1996: Had two assists and the last goal in a 6-1 victory at San Jose this season and moved past Delvecchio into second place on the Wings' all-time scoring list. Scotty Bowman congratulated Yzerman and, referring to Howe atop the list, kidded, "You only have a little bit more to go."

■ Feb. 19, 1997: Played in his 1,000th game, all with the Wings, and assisted on three goals in a 4-0 victory over Calgary at home.

1,000-GAME CLUB

In addition to Howe, Delvecchio and Yzerman, 13 players played in their 1,000th game while wearing a Wings jersey: Mike Ramsey, Ivan Boldirev, Dino Ciccarelli, Paul Coffey, Bernie Federko, Bill Gadsby, Terry Harper, Dave Lewis, Ted Lindsay, Brad Marsh, Brad McCrimmon, Brad Park and Dean Prentice.

different teams here."

Yzerman a Wing forever? It seemed unlikely in recent seasons, when he was dogged by trade rumors.

But keeping Yzerman in Detroit was owner Mike Ilitch's stated goal even in the wake of last season's disappointing playoff loss to Colorado.

"Steve Yzerman really wants to win, and he exemplifies that with his heart," Ilitch said.

"He played with as much heart as you can ask from a player.

"Steve is the ultimate team player. He played defensive hockey for the good of the team. He sacrificed stats and numbers to help the team win.

"People are always asking me, 'Who do you think are the great hockey players of all time?' " Ilitch said. "And I say they're the guys who can skate, shoot the puck, play defense, muck it up as rough as anybody, and not hang up at the blue line and cherry-pick.

"That's Steve Yzerman. With what he's accomplished in his career here, he probably rivals Gordie Howe more than

anybody I've ever seen."

Yzerman a Wing forever? Does he want that?

"Absolutely," the Captain said. "That's an easy goal for them, if they want to do that. I'm here as long as they want me."

On Nov. 15, 1996, they made it so when Yzerman agreed to a four-year, $17.5-million contract that includes a front-office job when his playing days are over.

"His professionalism, his approach to the game … not only is he a future Hall of Famer, he's so committed," Brendan Shanahan said.

Yzerman is the first player since Boston defenseman Ray Bourque on Feb. 8, 1993, to play 1,000 regular-season games with the same team.

When he accomplished the feat, Yzerman was well aware that he still had no Stanley Cup while Bourque had none in his 18th season.

Not that Yzerman was resigned to that fate.

"I still think I've got lots of hockey left," he said. "I still hope and expect to win a Stanley Cup in Detroit."

Says veteran defenseman Larry Murphy of coming from the last-place Toronto Maple Leafs to the Wings: "It's the biggest jump in the standings I've ever seen."

Dealing for defense

In Murphy, Wings get what they have needed

By Helene St. James
and Jason La Canfora

It was no secret that the Red Wings needed help on defense, and had for some time. Consider:

Mike Ramsey retired after the 1995-96 season, and Marc Bergevin signed as a free agent with St. Louis.

Vladimir Konstantinov suffered a severed left Achilles tendon playing tennis in the off-season and got off to a slow start.

Slava Fetisov would turn 39 before the season was over.

Paul Coffey was sent to Hartford with Keith Primeau in the Brendan Shanahan trade.

Nicklas Lidstrom and Bob Rouse were back, but who else was there?

The Wings first gave opportunities to three rookie defensemen — Anders Eriksson, Jamie Pushor and Aaron Ward — and forward Mathieu Dandenault.

Highly touted Eriksson wound up back at Adirondack, and the Dandenault experiment failed, though he gave it a yeoman effort.

Pushor and Ward added size and physical play to the mix, but with spring fast approaching, the Wings still were looking for veteran help.

In February, coach Scotty Bowman called 36-year-old Ramsey, who was running a sporting goods store and playing in a senior league in suburban Minneapolis. Ramsey agreed to rejoin the team and give it one more whirl.

He practiced with the Wings for two weeks and played in games in Anaheim and San Jose, but decided he couldn't contribute. So he retired again.

"That's the agreement we had in the beginning," Bowman said. "If he didn't think he could do it in his own mind, he could get out or we could get out, whenever he decided. So he decided he had enough. He had a month to go, but he felt he couldn't help us enough to put in the time."

That was March 18, which also happened to be the trading deadline.

The Wings went shopping for a veteran defenseman again and came up with future Hall of Famer Larry Murphy, 36, from last-place Toronto.

Larry Murphy

They did not part with any player or draft pick to get Murphy, but agreed to pick up the remainder of his $2.35-million contract for this season and a portion of his $2.475-million salary for next season. He was the Leafs' highest-paid player.

"It's a great opportunity," said Murphy, who could have vetoed the trade. "It's the biggest jump in the standings I've ever seen."

Detroit is the sixth stop in 17 seasons for 6-foot-2, 210-pound Murphy. He has been a second-team All-Star three times, most recently in 1995. But he was booed frequently at Maple Leaf Gardens this season and often was criticized for his lack of speed and his play in the defensive zone.

"I had him in Pittsburgh," Bowman said. "He's won two Canada Cups and two Stanley Cups. He's a very exciting power-play player. He's just an experienced defenseman. He's very strong offensively."

For his career, Murphy has 254 goals, 797 assists and 1,051 points — one point behind Denis Potvin for third place among defensemen.

Help is on the way

In addition to Larry Murphy, the Red Wings made two major acquisitions during the season:

Tomas Sandstrom

The Red Wings added Swedish forward Tomas Sandstrom in their continuing quest to get bigger and meaner for the playoffs.

Acquired Jan. 27 from the Pittsburgh Penguins for center Greg Johnson, Sandstrom embodies the concept of speaking softly off the ice and carrying a big stick on it.

He has a mean streak that often flares when he's parked in front of the opponent's net, where he uses his stick to create room.

"You always like to have players that are difficult to play against, and he's a guy who gets under your skin," left wing Brendan Shanahan said.

During the regular season, Sandstrom had 18 goals and 42 points, including nine goals and 18 points in 34 games with the Wings.

But it wasn't just his size — 6-feet-2 and 205 pounds — that excited the Wings about Sandstrom. They also liked his playoff history; he had 32 goals and 77 points in 115 games with the New York Rangers, Los Angeles and Pittsburgh.

"I'm aware of the pressure in Detroit," Sandstrom said, "but I don't think it's just on my shoulders. But, sure, I would like to win a Stanley Cup. I think Detroit has a good chance."

Joe Kocur

Want to talk tough?

"My role hasn't changed in the 12 years I've played in this league," Joe Kocur said. "It's to be a physical player and do what I do."

Just when it seemed as if his NHL career might be over, the Wings signed the enforcer Dec. 28, a week after his 32nd birthday. Kocur, who played for the Wings in 1984-91 and won a Stanley Cup with the Rangers in 1994, was cut by the Vancouver Canucks after last season.

"When you're sitting at home for nine months, there's self-doubt that creeps in," he said. "But I was working out six days a week for one reason and for one reason only. And it wasn't to look good in the summer."

Kocur played in senior leagues and in Wings alumni games, and was home for Christmas after playing five games with San Antonio of the IHL when coach Scotty Bowman called.

In his second game back, Kocur got into a fight with his former Bruise Brother, Bob Probert of the Chicago Blackhawks.

"I got to earn the respect that I once had," Kocur said. "Whether other teams feel the same way ... it's just something I got to do."

By Helene St. James

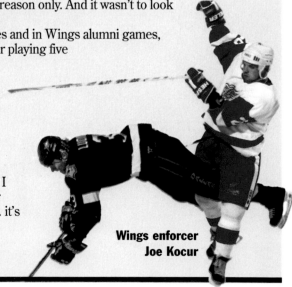

Wings enforcer Joe Kocur

Colorado's Claude Lemieux busted Kris Draper's face in the playoffs last season. Payback came in the form of a brawl at the Joe on March 26. In one of many fisticuffs, a shirtless Brent Severyn punches Aaron Ward.

Vengeance at last

Things get bloody
as McCarty leads the
effort to get even
with Claude Lemieux

*March 26 — If Red Wings fans
remember any night from the regular
season, it surely was this one, when the
Colorado Avalanche came to town.*

By Jason La Canfora

There was a hockey game to be
played, to be won this Wednesday
night. But the Red Wings took care
of some old business first.

It started with a scrum late in the first
period, and the Wings started pairing off
with Colorado players.

Lo and behold, Darren McCarty found

a dance partner in Claude Lemieux, who
broke Kris Draper's face 10 months
earlier with a check from behind. And, to
this day, Lemieux had shown no remorse
for it.

"I guess it was a payback," McCarty
said. "An opportunity presented itself, and
something happened."

"Something" was a bloody pummeling
of the Avalanche's Lemieux, Public
Enemy No. 1 in Hockeytown.

McCarty started the tango when he
spun away from a linesman and
coldcocked Lemieux. Lemieux fell to his
knees, fans jumped to their feet, and it was

Fight Night at Joe Louis Arena.

McCarty whacked Lemieux again with a left, and when Lemieux assumed the turtle position while holding his bleeding face, McCarty held him by the back of the neck with one hand and pummeled him with the other, throwing punches that appeared to have the force of the entire, roaring building behind them.

Before he was done, McCarty would drag Lemieux, stunned and bloody, to the Wings' bench, where Draper watched.

"Mac is such a team guy and he wanted to stick up for me," Draper said. "I consider us best friends, and I was happy he did what he did for me."

So was it over — the Lemieux affair? Yes, Draper said, and that left only a game to be decided.

Between the fights and pileups that continued for two periods, when there wasn't blood on the ice and players exchanging blows, on the rare occasions there wasn't chaos, there was hockey.

It was in those moments that the Wings showed they could beat — as well as beat up — the defending Stanley Cup champions.

The Wings showed guts, skill and resilience to erase a two-goal third-period deficit for a 6-5 victory on an overtime goal by, who else, McCarty.

"That was a great game," McCarty said. "That's one to remember. We stuck together in all aspects of our game. That's old-time hockey. That's the fun stuff."

McCarty's goal 39 seconds into overtime ended Colorado's four-game winning streak over the Wings.

"I don't think it could happen to a better guy," Draper said of his friend.

The Avalanche coaches and players were incensed after the game. Coach Marc Crawford even elbowed Wings defenseman Aaron Ward and tried to barge into the officials' locker room.

"I think that team has no heart," alternate captain Mike Keane said of the Wings. "Detroit had the opportunity to do that in our building, but they didn't. …

"I think they showed their true colors tonight. Everyone is gutless on that team, and I'd love to see them in the playoffs."

Be careful what you wish for …

It was as if two separate events occurred. One was a mix of grace, speed and dexterity; the other was a display of

STOP, DROP AND FIGHT

On this side of the blue line, wearing red and white trunks, Detroit's own — heavyweight Darren McCarty.

On the other side, in burgundy and gray, Colorado's deadweight — Claude Lemieux.

Oh, and over here it's 5-foot-9 Mike Vernon slugging 6-foot Patrick Roy. And, whoa! Igor Larionov vs. Peter Forsberg. And, and …

That was the card for the main event in the Thrilla at the Joe, a game that lasted nearly 3½ hours.

"By far it's the funnest game I've played in in years," Wings forward Kirk Maltby said. "Personally, I had a big smile on my face watching the goalies fighting and watching little Mike hold his own.

"I was surprised it went on for as long as it did, but the emotion was so high."

So high that referee Paul Devorski called enough penalties to fill two scoring sheets.

And there were more bouts: Brendan Shanahan vs. Adam Foote; Vladimir Konstantinov vs. Adam Deadmarsh; Jamie Pushor vs. Brent Severyn; Maltby vs. Rene Corbet; Aaron Ward vs. Severyn; Tomas Holmstrom vs. Mike Keane; McCarty vs. Deadmarsh, Pushor vs. Uwe Krupp.

"When you go through war," McCarty said, "Sometimes you need a little feistiness. To see Vernie in there slugging away, that's great."

When Lemieux crumbled to the ice at the start of a 10-minute brawl, Shanahan took a flying leap at Roy, who had left his crease to confront McCarty.

"I don't know what to say about that," Shanahan said. "There was a little WWF from both of us there. I saw Patrick going for McCarty, and I didn't want him to sneak up on him, so I went after him.

"When I was three feet in the air, I was thinking, 'What am I doing?' When I was five feet in the air, I said, 'What am I really doing here?' "

By Helene St. James

Claude Lemieux's "turtle" defense doesn't matter to Darren McCarty. His hits just keep on coming.

You know it's a crazy night when the goalies are fighting. Mike Vernon and Patrick Roy get their licks in.

Linesman Dan Schachte sends a bloody Patrick Roy to his bench.

At left:
Darren McCarty adds insult to the Avalanche's injuries as he scores the winner in overtime.

Below:
The Wings celebrate behind the net of a dejected Roy.

The rivalry's brief history

The faces tell the story ...

Steve Yzerman

Bob Rouse

Kris Draper

How did the Wings-Avalanche thing grow into such a rivalry so fast? Here are the events leading up to the March 26 Massacre:

■ **OCT. 6, 1995:** Transplanted from Quebec, Colorado beat the Wings, 3-2, in season opener at Denver.

■ **DEC. 2, 1995:** The Wings did the Avalanche a favor with an 11-1 win at Montreal. Patrick Roy, upset he hadn't been taken out soon enough, threw a fit on the Canadiens' bench and subsequently was traded to Colorado.

■ **MARCH 22, 1996:** The Wings beat the Avs, 7-0, and won the season series, 3-1.

■ **MAY 23, 1996:** In Game 3 of the Western Conference finals, Slava Kozlov slammed Avs defenseman Adam Foote's head into the glass, opening a cut. Claude

Lemieux got even later by sucker-punching Kozlov and opening a 10-stitch cut. After dropping the first two games at home, the Wings won, 6-4, at Denver.

■ **MAY 24, 1996:** Lemieux was suspended for one game after Wings coach Scotty Bowman asked the NHL to review the tape. An angry Avs coach Marc Crawford said Bowman "thinks so much, the plate in his head causes interference in our headsets," referring to a career-ending injury Bowman suffered in juniors.

■ **MAY 25, 1996:** Lemieux sat out Game 4, a 4-2 Avs victory.

■ **MAY 27, 1996:** Lemieux returned for Game 5 in Detroit, but the Wings won, 5-2, for a 3-2 series deficit.

■ **MAY 29, 1996:** In Game 6 at Denver, Lemieux boarded Kris Draper from

behind, causing severe facial injuries. Lemieux was ejected, but the Avs clinched the series, 4-1, and the Wings were left vowing revenge.

■ **NOV. 13, 1996:** Lemieux wasn't around for the first meeting this season because of abdominal surgery, and the Avs looked like Stanley Cup champs in a 4-1 victory at the Joe.

■ **DEC. 17, 1966:** Still no Lemieux, but Rene Corbet and Alexei Gusarov were carried off with concussions after hits by Aaron Ward and Martin Lapointe. "As far as I'm concerned, they can't moan about the Draper hit anymore," Foote said after the 4-3 Avs victory at home.

■ **MARCH 16, 1997:** Lemieux and Draper finally met again at McNichols Arena. But Lemieux escaped unscathed, and the Wings lost a penalty-filled game, 4-2.

---

pure brawn. The Wings won both. Both events left the crowd thoroughly satisfied.

There were 60 minutes in penalties and five fights in the first period — and a goal for good measure. Valeri Kamensky one-timed a blur past Wings goaltender Mike Vernon's right shoulder.

Sergei Fedorov, playing defense instead of his usual forward position, tied it 35 seconds into the second period. Fedorov, paired with Larry Murphy, whipped a wrist shot past Patrick Roy for his 29th goal of the season and first in three games.

"I thought he was excellent," coach Scotty Bowman said of Fedorov. "He played a terrific game offensively and defensively. We'll see if we can continue the experiment."

Kamensky beat Vernon again 1:12 into the period, and Martin Lapointe tied it again at 3:08. The Avs took a 4-2 lead on goals by Rene Corbet and Adam Deadmarsh.

Most of the time, such a lead would be insurmountable; Colorado entered the game 32-2-3 when leading after two periods. But what the Avalanche faced was an old-time team playing old-time hockey in front of fans seeking revenge. My, how they got it!

The Wings cut it to 4-3 when Nick Lidstrom spanked the puck from the left point past Roy with 19.1 seconds left in the period.

They kept the pressure on Roy in the opening moments of the third, sending pucks barely high and wide of the goal. At the other end, however, Kamensky

finished his hat trick and appeared to finish off the Wings 1:11 into the period.

But no letdown this night.

Lapointe buried a loose puck at 8:27 to bring the Wings within one, registering his first career two-goal game. Only 36 seconds later, Brendan Shanahan ended a game's worth of frustration.

Shanahan, stymied on three beautiful chances in the first period, beat Roy by flipping a puck off the back of the goalie's leg and into the net for a 5-5 tie.

It was Shanahan again in overtime, hitting McCarty with a pass at the side of the crease for the winning score.

"This was a game that brought the Wings together," said Vernon, who got his 300th career victory. "We can really build on this win as a team."

Stumbling through the stretch

Instead of high gear, they're stuck in third

By Steve Schrader

Was this a team that looked ready for the playoffs? Not the Red Wings in the final few weeks of the season.

"We've stunk lately," admitted Darren McCarty, who like everyone else blamed the lack of emotion and intensity on being stuck in the third spot in the conference with no place to go.

"Our team played a lot of nights as if everyone had the night off," said Brendan Shanahan, who finished the season with 47 goals.

The Wings finished with a 2-3-3 run. Not terrible, but not exactly building steam for the playoffs either.

Consider the strange goings-on of the final weeks of the season.

■ The Red Wings suddenly showed a taste for overtime, often because they lost third-period leads. At one point they played five straight overtime games, and seven of eight.

The good news was they won three of those overtime games and lost only one.

The Wings' offense also was struggling, scoring two or fewer goals in six of the final 10 games.

Coach Scotty Bowman chose to look on the bright side: "I'm just glad we're not getting into shootouts. Teams are tightening up, what else can I say?"

■ Sergei Fedorov, once one of the league's fastest-rising stars, a former 50-goal scorer, already had found himself bounced to a checking line.

Now he found himself on the blue line, paired with Larry Murphy, ostensibly to give Fedorov more ice time and the Wings a puck-carrying defenseman.

Two games into the experiment — which began March 26 in that fateful Colorado game — Fedorov put on a happy face about the change: "I get a lot of ice time. It seems I play like every other shift.

Things did not go swimmingly for coach Scotty Bowman, above, and his Wings during the final games of the regular season. He had put Sergei Fedorov on defense, which often put Fedorov, opposite, on his backside.

I feel good playing with Larry. He has a lot of experience and I can learn from him."

But as the playoffs approached and Bowman still had him on defense, the smile became a little more forced.

"I was thinking, 'Why the blue line?' But I don't think that anymore," Fedorov said. "I'm getting a lot of ice time. I don't want to stir the pot. It doesn't matter whether I'm happy or not. It's about what the team needs. Whatever the team needs, I'll do it."

■ Ice time was an issue with the goalies, too.

Chris Osgood was No. 1 during the season and played most of the games, but Bowman said he wanted two goalies ready for the playoffs.

Osgood and Mike Vernon expected to time-share in the postseason, and Bowman gave indications that would be the case, at least for starters: "Maybe eventually you go to one guy, maybe in the later rounds."

Bowman alternated the two from Feb. 1 until March 12, when Vernon suffered a knee injury. He made a shaky comeback March 23, giving up three goals on four shots against Chicago before being replaced by Kevin Hodson.

With only 10 games left in the season, Bowman still wanted to get Vernon back in shape and started him the next three games.

Osgood didn't start a game for 10 days, then started four straight, then Vernon for two, then Osgood again for the season finale …

So who would start the playoffs?

"We don't know," Osgood said. "He'll probably take it game by game like he did last year. I don't even worry about it, to tell you the truth. It's not even a thought in my mind right now.

"It's the same thing, anyways. We've never known in four years. It's his decision. He'll probably end up using both of us like last year."

■ After 81 games, the Wings still had a lot of questions about their own team. But one question would be answered by Game 82: Who their first-round playoff opponent would be.

The 1996-97 finale was an April 13 matinee against St. Louis at Joe Louis Arena. If the Blues won or tied, they would clinch the sixth seed in the Western Conference and play No. 3 Detroit in the first round.

In truth the Wings really didn't mind if that happened, because the Blues didn't seem that tough, and the travel certainly would be easier than Edmonton, the other option.

And the Wings played like it, losing a lackluster 3-1 effort. They finished 38-26-18, second to Dallas in the Central Division and third in the conference, a far cry below their record-setting season of 1995-96.

"We played really poorly," Steve Yzerman said of the season finale. "That was a really mediocre effort. I don't expect us to play that way in the playoffs.

"I'm expecting us to play well and I'm expecting us to win."

Other Wings agreed: Bring on the Blues.

"Absolutely," Doug Brown said. "The playoffs are a special time. It's what we're geared up for all year. There will be a higher level of intensity, you can't help it."

"You'll see a totally different team in the playoffs, for sure," Martin Lapointe said.

We'll see.

Seasonally

And here's how the 1996-97 Red Wings compare with the previous season's record-setting bunch:

■ **RECORD: Then** — 62-13-7. **Now** — 38-26-18. The Wings went from setting an NHL record for victories to their lowest win total for a full season since 34 in 1990-91. But they tied the team record for ties.

■ **POINTS: Then** — 131. **Now** — 94. That's a drop-off of 37, but as the Wings proved, the regular season doesn't mean anything.

■ **GOALS: Then** — 325. **Now** — 253. A deficit of almost a goal a game, but scoring was down all around the league.

■ **GOALS-AGAINST: Then** — 181 (2.21). **Now** — 197 (2.40). A slight increase, but if scoring is down …

Individually, Chris Osgood went from 2.17 to 2.29, and Mike Vernon from 2.26 to 2.43.

Chris Osgood, the Wings' No.1 goalie during the season, wasn't sure what his role would be in the playoffs.

■ **FINISH: Then** — first overall. **Now** — third in conference, fifth overall.

■ **LEADING SCORER: Then** — Sergei Fedorov, with 39 goals and 68 assists for 107 points. **Now** — Brendan Shanahan, with 47-41—88. That's the lowest total since Doug Shedden's 34-37—71 in 1985-86.

■ **PLUS-MINUS: Then** — Vladimir Konstantinov led with a plus-60, and only two Wings were minus players. **Now** — Konstantinov led with a plus-38, and the Wings had nine minus players.

■ *Note — When we say "lowest since," we're not counting the 48-game lockout season in 1995.*

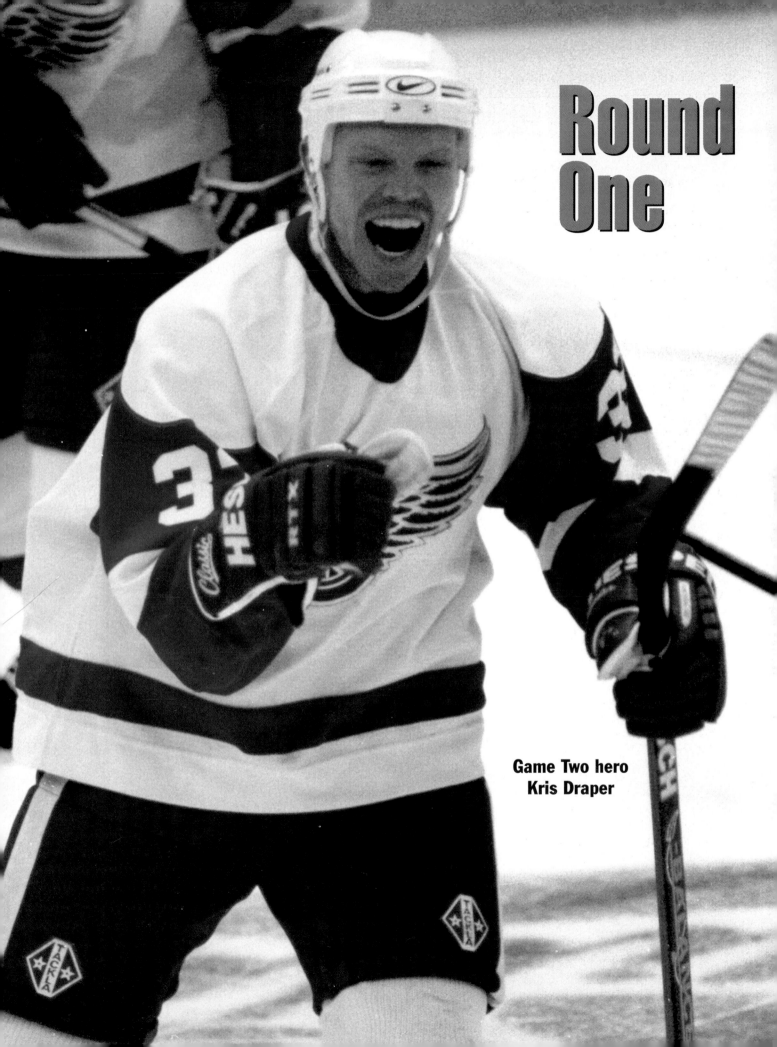

Round One

Game Two hero Kris Draper

Paying the penalties

The Wings put the puck to Grant Fuhr 30 times in Game One, but none got past him in his fourth career playoff shutout.

Wings take too many as offense sputters

ROUND ONE
GAME ONE

Wednesday, April 16

So the third-place Red Wings began another quest for their first Stanley Cup since 1955, this time more as a hopeful than a favorite. The first obstacles: sixth-place St. Louis and goalie Grant Fuhr.

By Jason La Canfora

There were no excuses in the Red Wings' dressing room. The reasons for their 2-0 loss to St. Louis at Joe Louis Arena, the first time they had been shut out in a series opener since 1950, were too glaring.

The Wings compromised their discipline by taking 10 penalties, several of them retaliatory. They failed to convert on seven power plays and couldn't create scoring chances.

"We just had to kill too many penalties," Wings coach Scotty Bowman said of his 2,000th game behind the bench, counting regular season and playoffs. "You can't win a game like that. … It's mainly retaliatory, and if you do that in this league you're going to get penalized."

And the Wings did, over and over again. They were called for double minors. They had to kill off five-on-three advantages.

Making matters worse, the Red Wings were in an 0-for-25 power-play slump over four games, including 0-for-16 in their last two games against the Blues.

"We didn't play totally disciplined," Joe Kocur said. "When you fall behind, it's awfully tough to come back shorthanded."

The Blues' Chris Pronger takes a shot at flattening Brendan Shanahan's
face as Stephane Matteau helps keep Shanahan defenseless.

Get down!

After great playoff slogans the past couple of years — remember "A Call to Arms"? — the Red Wings introduced their new rallying cry and theme song amid the usual pregame hoopla: "Get Up!!"

Huh?

"It's about the passion for Red Wings hockey that culminates around playoff time," marketing director Ted Speers said. "It refers to the pulling together of the Detroit community and hockey fans to get behind the team.

"It taps into the resurgence of the city and waking up with sweaty palms on game day. It expands on the aura of Hockeytown."

Sweaty palms?

Anyway, "Detroit Rock City" by Kiss was the inspiration for "Get Up!!"

Listen up:

Get up!
Everybody's gonna move their feet.
Get down!
Everybody's gonna leave their
 seat.
You gotta lose your mind in
 Detroit Rock City.

And so on.

"Get Up!!" might not have had the pizzazz of previous slogans, but it had a few things going for it:

■ The players liked it. They were given input on the new theme after being embarrassed by the previous year's "I Want Stanley."

■ It had a good beat.

■ It worked.

"Get Up!!" is available on CD and includes "Hockeytown" and the U.S. and Canadian national anthems by Detroit's own Karen Newman.

The Wings' offense was stagnant against a Blues team content, if not perfectly happy, to kick the puck, dump the puck, ice the puck, especially after taking the lead on first-period goals by Geoff Courtnall and Pierre Turgeon. Just get it out of their zone. Clutch, grab, hook. If the puck was in the neutral zone, they'd throw it to the corners.

When pucks got through the Blues' trap, Grant Fuhr was there to stop them, all 30 of them, for his fourth career playoff shutout.

"We need more traffic in front," said Sergei Fedorov, who opened the playoffs as a defenseman. "We didn't get enough scoring chances."

The Wings tried everything.

The Russian Five unit was dredged up on a late power play but couldn't produce a shot. Fedorov skated at forward briefly, still no goals.

Just more frustration, less discipline and a one-game deficit.

Red light, green light

Draper in driver's seat as Wings run down Fuhr

Friday, April 18

Down, 1-0, to St. Louis, Scotty Bowman decided it was time to implement Plan B for Game 2: Move Sergei Fedorov back to offense and play rookie defensemen Jamie Pushor and Aaron Ward.

By Jason La Canfora

In one moment, an entire series changed. The Red Wings hadn't scored in nearly 133 minutes against St. Louis, beginning with the regular-season finale. Goalie Grant Fuhr had stopped 53 consecutive shots in the playoffs.

Trailing, 1-0, on former Wing Marc Bergevin's goal, the Wings were on the verge of heading to St. Louis needing to win four of five games to survive.

Enter Kris Draper. Mr. Playoffs. Mr. April.

Draper tied Game 2 with a shorthanded goal early in the third period. Defenseman Larry Murphy gave the Wings a 2-1 lead three minutes later, and the score held as they evened the first-round series at one game each.

"We were wondering if we were ever going to score," Murphy said.

"It was a piano off 20 guys' backs," said Brendan Shanahan, who assisted on Draper's goal.

Draper was plugging away, killing a penalty, when Igor Kravchuk gave him room to the outside — just enough to get his legs pumping, to use his speed.

He came in on Fuhr, used Kravchuk as a screen, and shot with no particular target in mind. The puck whipped between Fuhr's pads and, finally, the light came on.

Vladimir Konstantinov gets more than a piece of Grant Fuhr, left.

Kris Draper, right, takes a victory lap after bringing the Joe Louis crowd to its feet with his game-tying goal.

ROUND ONE
GAME TWO

Joe Louis Arena erupted.
So did Draper.

He cruised behind the goal, plummeted to his knees at full speed and slid along the boards out to the red line, where his teammates awaited.

"When you don't score a lot of them, it's a little more exciting," Draper said. "I'm sure Shanny … doesn't get excited as much as Kris Draper, an eight-goal scorer."

Three minutes later, Murphy jumped on a Fuhr rebound and scored. High, glove side, more hysteria.

But the Wings kept the crowd chewing on fingernails for the final 12:51. First came a penalty for too many men on the ice. Then Sergei Fedorov drew a four-minute high-sticking penalty.

But outstanding penalty-killing and Mike Vernon's glove hand held the lead, even during a 1:16 two-man disadvantage. The Blues finished 0-for-8 on the power play.

For most of the game, it seemed there would be no joy in Hockeytown.

The Wings tried anything to get that first goal. Coach Scotty Bowman moved

Fedorov all over the ice and made sweeping line changes. He dressed seven defensemen. He gave the Russian Five another go at it.

But all they needed was Draper.

Physical challenge

Captain gets crunched, but Blues take the fall

Sunday, April 20

The series shifted to St. Louis with the Red Wings intent on learning their lessons from the first two games.

By Jason La Canfora

S teve Yzerman wouldn't strike back. The Blues threw elbows and forearms and hacked at him with sticks, but the Red Wings captain wouldn't budge. They ran him early and they ran him late, and Yzerman absorbed it all, too smart to retaliate.

He won with his will and he won with his hands, deflecting a shot for the winning goal in a 3-2 victory at the Kiel Center — and a 2-1 lead in the series.

"You can't take penalties," Yzerman said. "You'll kill your momentum. You just can't take penalties."

Tell the Blues, who gave up nine power plays on 10 penalties and sat in the penalty box for 16:32.

The Wings snapped an 0-for-17 playoff slump with the man advantage (0-for-35 beginning in the regular season) with power-play goals by Brendan Shanahan and Yzerman.

"It was definitely a relief to get one on the power play," defenseman Larry Murphy said, "a relief and a surprise."

The afternoon's first surprise came at 2:40, when Kris Draper gave the Wings the first goal of the game for the first time in the series.

The Wings outplayed the Blues in the first period but entered the dressing room tied at 1 when Nick Lidstrom's errant pass ended up on Brett Hull's stick for a wicked slap shot.

Yzerman, Shanahan and the coaches spoke up between periods.

"We knew we had them a little bit rattled, and Yzerman and Shanahan spoke up," associate coach Barry Smith said.

GAME THREE

"They said, 'Let's turn the other cheek, boys.' And we did. … Take a hit for the team and give hits."

Thirty-nine seconds into the second period, the Wings crashed the net and Shanahan poked home a loose puck for a 2-1 lead. But Joe Murphy beat Mike Vernon with a slap shot 6:36 into the second period for another tie.

But stupidity reigned for the Blues. Rookie Jim Campbell, playing in his first playoff game, went to the box with 5 1/2 minutes left in the second period for a cross-check away from the play.

Yzerman deflected Lidstrom's blast past Grant Fuhr on the power play.

"You can't justify it," Blues center Craig MacTavish said. "Penalties … ultimately cost us the hockey game."

But that's only half the story.

The other half lies in Yzerman's heart and mind and on his stick.

Geoff Courtnall takes a seat in front of Mike Vernon's crease. Vernon stopped 15 shots in a scoreless third period.

Opportunity missed, series extended

Fuhr pitches another shutout to make it 2-all

ROUND ONE
GAME FOUR

Tuesday, April 22

With a 2-1 series lead, the Red Wings seemed to overcome their fear of Fuhr. Then came Game 4 in St. Louis.

By Jason La Canfora

It wasn't what the Red Wings wanted. They could have taken a 3-1 lead against St. Louis and perhaps grabbed some rest between rounds.

But the Blues' 4-0 victory Tuesday at the Kiel Center assured at least a six-game series and a return to St. Louis.

"Three-one is a big difference from 2-2," captain Steve Yzerman said. "Obviously, we missed a great opportunity."

Blues goalie Grant Fuhr stopped 28 shots for his fifth career playoff shutout and second of the series.

"We knew we had to have this game, and everybody played like we had to have it," Fuhr said.

Wings goalie Mike Vernon, Fuhr's rival for a decade, was often left to fend for himself. After allowing four goals on 23 shots, Vernon was replaced with 10:37 left by Chris Osgood, making his first appearance of the playoffs.

"I had no complaints (with Vernon)," coach Scotty Bowman said. "I just wanted to give him a rest."

Geoff Courtnall scored twice, including a goal that gave St. Louis a 3-0 lead 1:10 into the third period. Brett Hull (three assists) and Pavol Demitra (one goal, two assists) each had three points.

Igor Larionov leads the Wings with three points — in the entire series.

"We've got to look in the mirror and take it upon yourself," said 47-goal scorer Brendan Shanahan. "When we get shut out, players like myself take it personally."

The Blues wanted this game more. At

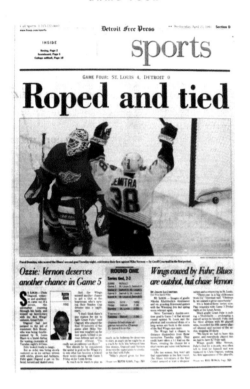

least they played that way.

For the first time in the series, the Wings were reduced to dumping and flipping the puck from their zone to relieve pressure. Vernon was frequently tested.

Frustration set in, and Vernon was the victim. Courtnall was alone for his second goal of the game, and no one put a body on Chris Pronger for the Blues' fourth goal, at 9:23 of the third.

"All of a sudden we started taking unnecessary chances," Shanahan said. "We left our game plan and they started getting three-on-ones."

After Vernon was yanked, and following a five-on-five melee, Osgood was pulled for an extra attacker. But the Wings couldn't score with a six-on-three advantage.

In a word ...

In a word ...

Many Red Wings say the first turning point in the playoffs — perhaps the most important — came in the locker room after the Game 4 loss in St. Louis.

After another shutout loss, Red Wings captain Steve Yzerman demanded his teammates' attention.

Yzerman usually leads by example, but not when he's upset with his production. He was moved to speak, to vow to do better, to demand more from his fellow star teammates.

The message was delivered calmly — yet sternly — for about 10 minutes in the locker room after a 4-0 loss in St. Louis on April 22. The Wings listened intently with the sweat of Game 4 still dripping from their brows.

Their captain didn't want them to forget the hollow feeling of not taking command of their first-round series and of not giving a full effort.

"We've just got to play harder," Yzerman said the next day. "Our top players have got to play harder. We've got to produce and lead the team."

Yzerman totaled one point in the first four games; Brendan Shanahan had two. Sergei Fedorov and Darren McCarty were scoreless.

As a team, the Wings had five goals in four games and were shut out twice.

"Our top guys have to step up," Shanahan said. "Chances are great, but it's time that we produce. Chances aren't good enough.

"Stevie talked about it after the game. We have to put more pressure on ourselves as go-to guys to step up."

Coach Scotty Bowman's advice was simple: No more posts. No more miscues. Just "put 'em in" — starting with Yzerman, Shanahan and Fedorov.

"Steve said the top guys have got to do more and pick up their level of the game," Martin Lapointe said. "Everyone has respect for what he was saying. They'll get going. I'm not worried about that."

By Jason La Canfora

Soviet reunion

Bowman lets Russians come out and play

Friday, April 25

The Red Wings indeed came to life, sparked by their Captain's suggestion that their stars start producing and by the revival of the Russian Five.

By Jason La Canfora

Hello, comrades, well hello, comrades. It's so nice to have you back where you belong. The Russian Unit is back. After four games of Red Wings coach Scotty Bowman's tinkering and decoying and teasing, he finally let them play in Game 5 against St. Louis.

And play they did. The skating, the stickhandling, the speed and the grace all returned with each shift together. Forwards Igor Larionov, Sergei Fedorov and Slava Kozlov, and defensemen Slava Fetisov and Vladimir Konstantinov were the difference in the Wings' 5-2 victory at Joe Louis Arena.

As a result, the Wings took a 3-2 series lead.

"Everybody was excited before the game when Scotty told us we were going to play together," Larionov said. "We know each other real well. We play the same hockey."

Blues goalie Grant Fuhr had a shaky start. The first two shots caught him off guard, but he stopped them. He wasn't prepared for the third, either.

Steve Yzerman's slap shot from 95 feet, one stride in from the red line, found its way into the net for a 1-0 lead.

The Wings were relentless, and the Blues had no offense — just three shots in the period. But it took only one to tie it after Martin Lapointe was called for

Somewhere in this cloud of snow is a St. Louis Blue, deposited there courtesy of Vladimir Konstantinov.

goalie interference.

Al MacInnis snuck in from the point on the power play and knocked in Brett Hull's cross-crease pass.

Five minutes into the second period,

Larionov navigated the neutral zone and found Kozlov in the slot for his first goal. After 29 shots in the series, one of the Russians finally had a goal.

"I love playing with the Russian Five," Kozlov said. "I missed the Russian Five, since we didn't play much in the regular season."

Less than three minutes later, Darren McCarty backhanded in the rebound for his first goal.

Blues rookie Jim Campbell scored on the power play and cut the deficit to 3-2, but the Wings weren't done.

Brendan Shanahan backhanded a loose puck past Fuhr for a 4-2 lead 13:15 into the second. Larry Murphy added a power-play goal in the third.

The Blues tried to intimidate the Russians with a scrum at the end of the second, but it didn't work. Fedorov put Scott Pellerin on his back twice.

"It felt great," Fedorov said. "You do that when you have to do that."

They did it all. A little bit of Moscow on the Detroit River.

The Grind Line

By Helene St. James

Their mission was simple: Crash and bang and frustrate the bad guys. Kris Draper, Kirk Maltby, Darren McCarty and Joe Kocur made up one of the Red Wings' best weapons in the playoffs: the Grind Line.

Think of New Jersey's Crash Line of Mike Peluso, Bobby Holik and Randy McKay, which helped frustrate the Wings for four miserable games in the Stanley Cup finals two years ago.

The Grind Line began with Draper centering Maltby and Kocur, then grew when McCarty took over Kocur's regular spot for the final two games against St. Louis. (Kocur still took some shifts.)

"We have a blast," said McCarty, 25. "Drapes is a talker out there, I just laugh. Malts will say stuff, too, but Drapes is the one who talks. We all yell at each other and yell at the other guys. I just watch and laugh at those two."

McCarty, who had been playing with Brendan Shanahan and Igor Larionov, enjoyed crashing and banging and hitting like the McCarty of old.

"That's the way I should play," he said. "I played with Drapes for a long time, and we always played well together, and Malts plays the same way. The first two guys forecheck and then the third guy picks up.

"Playing with Shanny, sometimes you get in there and make the prettiest play, and I got away from my game. Playing with these guys gets me back to that. It's basic hockey. No special plays, just bump and grind."

Nothing special? Just grind at full speed. Get the puck down low, throw it at the net. Score the odd goal. Hit. Hit some more. Draw penalties.

From left, Grinders Darren McCarty, Kris Draper, Kirk Maltby and Joe Kocur fit Red Wings' playoff hockey to a T ... as in the T-shirt below that features Maltby, Draper and Kocur.

"That's exactly what we want to do," said Draper, 25. "We can do some things out there, and we've been able to chip in offensively, too.

"We're not about pretty plays in the neutral zone. We want them to dump, so we can get a good forecheck on them. Along the boards, Mac, Malts and Joey are so strong that when the puck comes around the boards, you're always confident they can get it out. And I feel I can get in some footraces, and that's what I want to do."

And Kocur? He's the older, wiser voice of the line.

"We're not going to go out there and make the pretty plays the Larionovs and Yzermans are going to make," said Kocur, 32. "We have to go out there and create our own chances, and the best way to do that is turnovers by their defense and by getting in and being relentless on them.

"I'm just out there to have a calming effect on the other players."

The Grind Line.

It has spawned a T-shirt, made in the pre-McCarty days when it was Draper, Maltby and Kocur, and best described by Maltby as "one of those where our heads are big and whatnot; you can kind of see us. I got my visor on, so you can see that's me."

Good point. When reporters enter the locker room, they flock to Draper and McCarty. Kocur and Maltby get a few stragglers.

"I don't mind it," said Maltby, 24. "I can walk around and do whatever I want to do without getting harassed. Well, not harassed, but it doesn't bother me at all. If recognition comes along, that's fine."

The bad guys know who he is.

Taking care of business

Wings beat the Blues, but don't jump for joy

Sunday, April 27

The Red Wings needed one more victory to eliminate St. Louis and win their first-round series for the third straight year. That hadn't happened since 1954-56, their dynasty years.

By Jason La Canfora

ed Wings players spoke calmly in their designer suits after eliminating St. Louis in six games. They were relieved, happy and restrained. Ties were straight. Collars were buttoned. No beer covered heads; there were no champagne explosions. This was all business. One team down, three to go.

The 3-1 win at the Kiel Center was simply a means to an end — the only prize that matters is the Stanley Cup.

"We won the game; that's the best way to put it," veteran Joe Kocur said. "There wasn't any extra enthusiasm. Guys were happy to win the series and get ready to move on."

They are moving on because of more terrific goaltending from Mike Vernon (24 saves), an on-again/off-again power play, tenacious hustle from the grinders and the NHL's ridiculous in-the-crease rule.

Brett Hull gave the Blues the lead on their first shot, 2:12 into the game.

The Wings tied it on a power play at 8:45, when Vladimir Konstantinov darted past Grant Fuhr and created a screen for Slava Kozlov.

Kozlov ripped a shot between the goalie's pads for his second goal of the series, second on the power play and

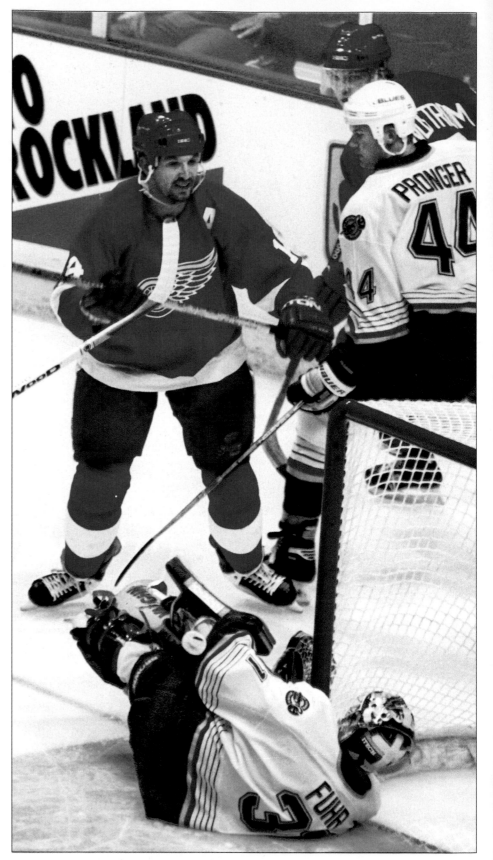

Brendan Shanahan beats Grant Fuhr to give the Wings a 2-1 lead in the second period. The goal turned out to be the series clincher.

The Blues' Brett Hull shakes hands with Wings goalie Chris Osgood, who played only 10 minutes in the series.

ROUND ONE
GAME SIX

second in as many games.

"Kozzie today played the best game I've ever seen him play," captain Steve Yzerman said.

Kozlov said: "My confidence was fine at the beginning of the playoffs, but I didn't have enough ice time playing on the third or fourth lines. That's why I didn't score more. I had no chances.

"Now I play with Russian Five. They pay attention to Igor and Sergei, so I have lots of room to skate."

Slava Fetisov was cross-checked in the face by Jim Campbell 29 seconds into the second period, and the Wings capitalized again.

Tomas Sandstrom picked up his first point by passing across the crease to Brendan Shanahan, who beat Fuhr high for a 2-1 lead.

St. Louis appeared to tie the game with 52.8 seconds left in the second.

Pierre Turgeon collected a gift bounce off the glass and put the puck past Vernon. But video replays showed his skate was in the crease.

No goal. No tie.

The Blues were irate, but in the twisted world of the NHL, it was the right call.

"They've got to really refine this rule," Wings coach Scotty Bowman said. "I would feel terrible if it happened to our team."

The Wings iced the game 8:24 into the third period when Kirk Maltby banged with two Blues defensemen to create a turnover, then headed straight for the net. Darren McCarty shot the loose puck on goal, and Maltby was in perfect position to put in the rebound.

The Wings killed the clock and went to the dressing room for a few pats on the back and quick showers. Savor the moment, get on the plane.

The journey was just beginning.

Detroit-St. Louis: First round
Composite Box Score

Detroit wins, 4-2 (home team in CAPITALS)

Date	Score	Goalies	Winning goal
April 16, 1997	Blues 2, WINGS 0	Vernon/Fuhr	Courtnall
April 18, 1997	WINGS 2, Blues 1	Vernon/Fuhr	Murphy
April 20, 1997	Wings 3, BLUES 2	Vernon/Fuhr	Yzerman
April 22, 1997	BLUES 4, Wings 0	Vernon, Osgood/Fuhr	Courtnall
April 25, 1997	WINGS 5, Blues 2	Vernon/Fuhr	McCarty
April 27, 1997	Wings 3, BLUES 1	Vernon/Fuhr	Shanahan

Scoring by period

	1st	2nd	3rd	OT	Total
Wings	3	6	4	0	13
Blues	8	2	2	0	12

Shots by period

	1st	2nd	3rd	OT	Total
Wings	56	66	61	0	183
Blues	38	50	61	0	149

Individual Scoring

	GP	G	A	Pts.	+/-	PM	PP	S	Pct.
Brendan Shanahan	6	3	3	6	2	12	2	24	12.5
Larry Murphy	6	2	3	5	1	4	1	16	12.5
Igor Larionov	6	0	5	5	-1	2	0	9	.0
Kris Draper	6	2	1	3	3	8	0	11	18.2
Steve Yzerman	6	2	1	3	E	4	1	18	11.1
Slava Kozlov	6	2	0	2	-2	8	2	9	22.2
Kirk Maltby	6	1	1	2	2	6	0	8	12.5
Darren McCarty	6	1	1	2	1	10	0	9	11.1
Sergei Fedorov	6	0	2	2	-2	10	0	20	.0
Martin Lapointe	6	0	2	2	1	21	0	8	.0
Nicklas Lidstrom	6	0	2	2	1	0	0	22	.0
Jamie Pushor	5	0	1	1	-1	5	0	3	.0
Joey Kocur	6	0	1	1	1	2	0	5	.0
Tomas Sandstrom	6	0	1	1	-4	14	0	10	.0
Tomas Holmstrom	1	0	0	0	-1	0	0	0	.0
Chris Osgood	1	0	0	0	2	0	0	.0	
Tim Taylor	1	0	0	0	E	0	0	0	.0
Aaron Ward	5	0	0	0	1	2	0	1	.0
Slava Fetisov	6	0	0	0	E	2	0	3	.0
Vlad. Konstantinov	6	0	0	0	-3	8	0	5	.0
Bob Rouse	6	0	0	0	2	29	0	2	.0

Power play: 6-for-42, 14.3%. **Penalty killing:** 32-of-37, 86.5%

Goaltending

	GP	MIN	GA	Avg.	EN	SO	W	L	Shots	Save%
Mike Vernon	6	348	12	2.07	0	0	4	2	145	.917
Chris Osgood	1	10	0	0.00	0	0	0	0	4	1.000

Individual Scoring

	GP	G	A	Pts.	+/-	PM	PP	S	Pct.
Brett Hull	6	2	7	9	4	2	0	25	8.0
Geoff Courtnall	6	3	1	4	E	23	1	11	27.3
Pavol Demitra	6	1	3	4	3	6	0	8	12.5
Al MacInnis	6	1	2	3	-1	4	1	22	4.5
Pierre Turgeon	5	1	1	2	E	2	1	8	12.5
Joe Murphy	6	1	1	2	-2	10	1	8	12.5
Chris Pronger	6	1	1	2	E	22	0	19	5.3
Jim Campbell	4	1	0	1	-1	6	1	6	16.7
Marc Bergevin	6	1	0	1	3	8	0	4	25.0
Chris McAlpine	4	0	1	1	1	0	0	6	.0
Craig MacTavish	1	0	0	0	-1	2	0	0	.0
Igor Kravchuk	2	0	0	0	-1	2	0	6	.0
Robert Petrovicky	2	0	0	0	1	0	0	1	.0
Sergio Momesso	3	0	0	0	E	6	0	0	.0
Stephane Matteau	5	0	0	0	E	0	0	2	.0
Mike Peluso	5	0	0	0	-1	25	0	1	.0
Harry York	5	0	0	0	-1	2	0	2	.0
Craig Conroy	6	0	0	0	-1	8	0	4	.0
Grant Fuhr	6	0	0	0		4	0	0	.0
Stephen Leach	6	0	0	0	-2	33	0	8	.0
Scott Pellerin	6	0	0	0	-1	6	0	7	.0
Ricard Persson	6	0	0	0	-2	27	0	1	.0
Tony Twist	6	0	0	0	0	0	0	0	.0

Power play: 5-for-37, 13.5%. **Penalty killing:** 36-of-42, 85.7%

Goaltending

	GP	MIN	GA	Avg.	EN	SO	W	L	Shots	Save%
Grant Fuhr	6	357	13	2.18	0	2	2	4	183	.929

Round Two

Mike Vernon
and
Brendan Shanahan

A change of fortune

Martin Lapointe, center, celebrates his game-winning goal with Darren McCarty, left, and Joe Kocur.

Fedorov, Lapointe put first feathers in their caps

Friday, May 2

The Wings had to wait to find out whom their second-round opponent would be — Dallas Stars, Anaheim or Phoenix. Edmonton eliminated the second-seeded Stars and the Mighty Ducks beat the Coyotes, both in seven-game series. So the Wings faced the Ducks, a team they hadn't beaten in the regular season.

By Jason La Canfora

There had to be another goal in Sergei Fedorov. There had to be another goal in Martin Lapointe.

Their bad luck couldn't have ended at a better time.

They scored the Red Wings' goals Friday night, the first for each in the playoffs. Fedorov's tied the game in the third period. Lapointe's won it 59 seconds into overtime. And Detroit beat Anaheim, 2-1, in Game 1 of the Western Conference semifinals.

Fedorov had one goal in his last 15 games and two in his last 25 playoff games. And the Wings had gone 145

minutes, 15 seconds without scoring against the Mighty Ducks this season until Fedorov broke the spell with 8:59 to play in the third period.

"I had eight shots and still not yet, still not yet," he said. "Then I just put the shot on goal, and all of a sudden I scored. Honestly, I wasn't sure if I was going to score (again) or not."

Half of Joe Louis Arena was still in line for hot dogs and beer when Lapointe began battling along the boards for the

The Mighty Ducks' Steve Rucchin moves in for an unsuccessful shot on Mike Vernon.

puck, then hit Brendan Shanahan with a pass through the neutral zone.

Everyone thought Shanahan would shoot — including goalie Guy Hebert, who cheated toward Shanahan coming to his right. But Shanahan passed to Lapointe for what he called his first overtime playoff goal at any level.

"I didn't even think. I just one-timed it," Lapointe said. "There's nothing like overtime, especially when you score the goal. You always want to be the hero."

The Wings had overcome a 1-0 deficit against a tight-checking, trapping team that had held them to three goals in four regular-season games (0-3-1).

Before Fedorov's goal, the Wings had scored three times on 158 shots against the Ducks this season. Nothing the Wings tried could foil Hebert.

"We're pretty happy with about 60 minutes of tonight," Hebert said. "One play, I guess, can kill you."

Actually, the Wings outplayed Anaheim throughout the game and produced more scoring chances. But the Ducks never pressed; they laid back, cleared the zone and dumped the puck.

The Wings did a tremendous job against Paul Kariya and Teemu Selanne, holding Kariya to one goal and Selanne to two third-period shots.

On this night, Fedorov was better than both of them.

On this night, no one was more of a

clutch player than Lapointe.

"It feels pretty good, but I can't get too excited," Lapointe said. "I'll enjoy it for now, but we've got another game Sunday, and it's bigger than this one."

A bigger game for sure, but it's hard to imagine a bigger goal.

Goosed!

Anaheim coach Ron Wilson was thrilled to be playing the Red Wings in the second round, and not because he had any score to settle.

Wilson, who was born in Windsor, was returning to Hockeytown, where his father, Larry, and uncle Johnny played and coached. Ron learned the game by hanging around the Olympia.

"It's very special for me," said Wilson, 41, who coached Team USA to the World Cup last summer. "My dad and my uncle began their careers in the Detroit system. They won Stanley Cups in Detroit. ... It's like destiny. I always wanted to beat the Red Wings to avenge my dad's and uncle's firing."

Then he laughed: "I'm going to straighten out our name in Detroit, one way or another."

Wilson had more than vengeance on his mind. He seemed to throw his hat in the ring, should the Wings coaching job become open. "It's always in the back of your mind, but it's not something I dwell on," he said. "You say, geez, that would be so neat to go back there because of where I grew up ...

"You could say in a perfect world the Detroit Red Wings would be a dream job for me because of my family background, but it's not something I covet right now. I'm only concerned with the Mighty Ducks."

Not anymore.

Shortly after the Ducks' playoff run, Wilson was fired.

By Jason La Canfora

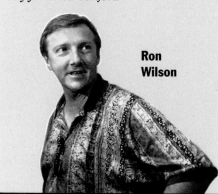

Ron Wilson

Over and over again

Wings prove they can go the distance

Sunday, May 4

The Wings got a taste of overtime in their first victory over Anaheim, but it was nothing compared to Game 2.

By Keith Gave

Another day, another overtime. And another and another. The Wings and Anaheim put on a magnificent performance Sunday, a 3-2 Detroit victory that ended with a triple-overtime goal by the quietest hero, Slava Kozlov.

His power-play goal on a slap shot ended the game five hours, 40 minutes and 122 shots after it began — 1:31 into the third overtime.

"No big deal," Kozlov said in a language he's still trying to master. "Not for Red Wings. We have good shape. We can play couple more overtimes. No problem."

As for the goal that gave the Wings a 2-0 series lead, Kozlov said: "Every goal is important. It's only two games. We need to win a couple of more, but we feel pretty comfortable now."

The Wings took a 1-0 lead at 4:34 of the second period when captain Steve Yzerman took a seemingly harmless shot, but defenseman J.J. Daigneault deflected it past goalie Guy Hebert.

Anaheim's Jari Kurri tied it at 4:18 of the third, but Doug Brown regained a 2-1 lead for Detroit at 12:14. That held up until Teemu Selanne forced overtime with 3:07 left.

Then the goaltenders took over — Mike Vernon for Detroit and Mikhail Shtalenkov, subbing admirably for Hebert, who left in the third period with a groin

It was a mob scene after Slava Kozlov blew the Ducks out of the water with a triple-overtime goal.

injury. And they played brilliantly until Kozlov beat his comrade.

"Yes, I know him from Russia," Kozlov said. Asked if he was aware of Shtalenkov's weaknesses, Kozlov smiled and said, "That is secret."

Here's one more secret: This series is anything but boring. Tight, certainly, and sometimes a bit conservative. But full of strategy and emotion to match some brilliant performances.

"It's a little bit of a chess match out there, certainly," said Brown, who drew the penalty in the third overtime that set up Kozlov's winner.

Until then, the game was a thriller, with both goalies making huge saves. Vernon — who energized between periods by

drinking half-and-half, Coke and water, and by eating oranges and bananas — matched Shtalenkov, big save for big save.

Shortly after Shtalenkov denied Larry Murphy on a good chance early in the first overtime, Vernon stopped Joe Sacco's shot from the high slot, then prevented Warren Rychel from jamming the puck in from the crease.

How about Sergei Fedorov swooping around the Anaheim net 19 seconds into the second OT, only to have his wraparound attempt smothered by Shtalenkov? Or Daigneault, in alone on Vernon at 8:46, faking a forehand and beating Vernon with a backhander that hit the left post?

It might be tight, defensive hockey. There might not be many goals. But it doesn't get much better than what the Wings and Ducks gave us Sunday — more than 100 minutes of a thrill ride they can't give you at Disneyland.

Most of the bounces went Mike Vernon's way in Game 2. He stopped 49 of 51 shots.

At left, the "Duck Hunters" declare open season on Anaheim.

A reason to smile

The perfect accessory – something in Brown

Tuesday, May 6

The Wings took their hard-earned 2-0 series lead to California, the land of 10:30 face-offs, warrior princesses and new heroes.

By Jason La Canfora

A week ago, Red Wings forward Doug Brown was wondering when he would play again. He watched the St. Louis series from the stands and press box.

Now he's all smiles. Brown is contributing every shift and making key plays against the Mighty Ducks. The last time he sat in the stands was at Dodger Stadium this week, and even then he caught a foul ball.

For the second straight game, Brown scored a key goal in the Wings' 5-3 comeback victory at the Pond in Anaheim

The traffic in California is notorious, but the jam in front of the Anaheim net was a spectacular pileup.

Wings goalie Mike Vernon tries to get back in position as Wings defenseman Vladimir Konstantinov just tries to get loose.

Lucy Lawless, moments before her unexpected revelation.

for a 3-0 series lead.

Life was good again.

"You just keep waiting for your chance," said Brown, 32. "You have to keep believing in yourself and working hard. You try to practice and show the coaches what you can do and hope your number is called.

Doug Brown

"It's awful sitting out. It's really hard. You've been playing this sport for 25 years. You play it because you love the game; you love to play; you love competing. You want to win the championship no matter what level it's at. It's tough being on the sidelines."

Slava Kozlov also continued his hot streak with two goals — his fifth in five games — and an assist.

The Ducks jumped to a 2-0 first-period lead on goals by stars Paul Kariya and Teemu Selanne while the Wings were down two men.

Kozlov cut it to 2-1 with a power play goal at 15:47.

Ted Drury restored Anaheim's two-goal lead early in the second period, but Igor Larionov made it 3-2 at 13:03.

With 3:32 seconds left in the period, Mikhail Shtalenkov yielded a long rebound. Tomas Sandstrom sent the puck on goal from the far boards, and Brown streaked in and drove it to the goalie's left for a 3-3 tie.

The Wings were buzzing now.

They outshot the Ducks, 23-6, in the second period and completed their comeback in the third.

Sergei Fedorov got behind Dan Trebil,

one of the Anaheim rookie's many costly mistakes, and beat Shtalenkov between his right pad and the post at 3:34.

About 20 seconds later, Fedorov passed to Kozlov, who finished a 90-foot breakaway with a backhand move, and the Wings had their first two-goal lead of the series.

"I'm so happy for Kozzie, because he was struggling all season long," Larionov said of Kozlov's hot streak. "He was kind of in the doghouse, but lately he has played the best hockey I've ever seen him play in Detroit.

"It's hard for a young guy sometimes. I just told him this is the time to play the great hockey he can play."

Oh, yes, we can see

What were people talking about the morning after the Red Wings' Game 3 victory in Anaheim?

The game, sure, but also "Xena: Warrior Princess." Lucy Lawless, star of the syndicated television program, wore a revealing costume with an Uncle Sam motif to sing the national anthem.

How revealing?

As she hit the final notes, Lawless threw open her blue blazer and, well, spilled out of the top of her costume for all of the television viewing audience to see.

The next day, Lawless pleaded ignorance during an interview with Dick Purtan on WOMC-FM (104.3).

"You mean I've been flashing on national TV?" she said. "I am horrified. It did not really come down, did it? Only a little popped out? Big deal."

When Purtan's crew described the incident in detail for her, Lawless said, "Oh, you lie. … I don't need that kind of publicity. I get plenty of attention as it is.

"That costume was too damn small. My mother will cry."

The Russian Five

Slava
Fetisov

Sergei
Fedorov

An iron curtain is wrapped around the Ducks

By Keith Gave

The yellow brick road ran into a dead end, at an Iron Curtain. The Mighty Ducks, who borrowed inspiration from "The Wizard of Oz," got a lesson in Stanley Cup hockey from a bunch of Russian imports.

The resurgent Russian Five scored six of the Wings' 13 goals in the four-game sweep of Anaheim, including four in the 5-3 victory in Game 3.

And their performance helped to bury a hideous myth about Russian players in the NHL, that they don't get up for the playoffs, that they don't know the meaning of the Stanley Cup.

Slava Fetisov, the elder statesman of the Russian Unit and former Red Army captain, shrugs off such suggestions as bigotry his comrades have to overcome.

"Look at me," Fetisov said. "I'm 39. It's probably much better for me to get season over as soon as possible to get rest. But we're playing for championship. We're winners. We all grew up with our national team, when anything but first place was a tragedy.

"The NHL is the same situation. Everybody wants to win this Cup and put their names on this trophy also. Russians are no exceptions."

Ah, but they're great targets for abuse in enemy arenas. As in St. Louis and Anaheim, where fans chanted "U-S-A! U-S-A!" when the Russian Five were weaving their magic.

"Yes, we hear it," defenseman Vladimir Konstantinov said. "What are they cheering that for? We just try to score a goal

Ducks goalie Mikhail Shtalenkov tries to fend off Sergei Fedorov.

right away, and get more attention from the stands."

In Game 3 against the Ducks, center Igor Larionov scored about 10 seconds after the chants started; they quickly died down. In St. Louis, Slava Kozlov scored his first of the playoffs during a chorus of "U-S-A!" as well.

Last season, the Russian Unit was ineffective in the playoffs and eventually disbanded. Coach Scotty Bowman hardly played the unit this season until the first-round series against St. Louis.

But wingers Sergei Fedorov and Kozlov played their best hockey of the season during the playoffs, thanks primarily to Larionov.

"He's like the hub on their wheel; he's the computer chip for them," said Anaheim coach Ron Wilson. "Igor has made

Vladimir Konstantinov   **Igor Larionov**   **Slava Kozlov**

Fedorov a better player again. He's a master at taking people out of position like a pied piper and getting the puck to the open man."

And one guy who was open a lot was Kozlov, at times the most invisible of the five Russians. That makes him the most dangerous when he asserts himself, as he did in the playoffs.

"See how Slava is playing now, compared to the regular season," Konstantinov said. "That's the best example. He raises his level several steps up."

Larionov, Kozlov's mentor, is delighted with his pupil's success.

"I'm so happy for Kozzie because he was struggling all season long," Larionov said. "He was kind of in the doghouse, but lately he has played the best hockey I've ever seen

him play in Detroit. It's hard for a young guy sometimes. I just told him this is the time to play the great hockey he can play."

The goals started coming in bunches, but the Kozlov's main goal was a Stanley Cup, and for more reasons than getting his own name on it.

He was acutely aware that an NHL championship was the only thing his two greatest heroes, Larionov and Fetisov, hadn't won in their careers.

"If we win Stanley Cup," Kozlov said, "maybe they put Igor and Slava in the museum in Toronto."

That would be the Hockey Hall of Fame, which only recently razed its own Iron Curtain and opened its doors to Russian stars as well.

Sweepy-eyed

Wings work late, but the overtime is nice

Thursday, May 8

One more victory in Anaheim and the Wings could fly home to Detroit with their third straight berth in the Western Conference finals. It turned out to be a red-eye.

By Jason La Canfora

While you were sleeping, the Red Wings were scarfing down bananas and water, preparing to play their fifth period of hockey.

While you were sleeping, Martin Lapointe was addressing his teammates between periods, urging a hero to step up.

While you were sleeping, Brendan Shanahan scored 17:03 into the second overtime, giving the Wings a 3-2 win and a four-game sweep of Anaheim.

The struggle began in regulation, when the Wings overcame two deficits.

The teams traded first-period goals by Joe Sacco and Doug Brown, but Brian Bellows gave the Mighty Ducks a 2-1 lead in the second.

Then it was up to Nick Lidstrom, who was stopped on his first 47 shots in the first nine games of the playoffs. But he never stopped pressing and tied the game at 9:09 of the third period.

2-2. Those numbers would lurk on the Pond's scoreboard for another 48 minutes of play. But an upbeat group of Wings headed off after the third period.

There was constant chatter in the dressing room, inspirational messages delivered between bites of orange wedges and bananas and gulps of water and Gatorade.

Vladimir Konstantinov keeps the Ducks' Mark Janssens in his place as Tim Taylor moves in to take control of the puck.

"We were happy to be going to overtime, because we were down twice during the game," Brown said. "We've been in overtime a lot during the season and obviously in the playoffs. We were confident."

By the end of the first OT, the Wings had peppered goalie Mikhail Shtalenkov with 57 shots (he went on to make a franchise-record 70 saves).

Back to the dressing room. More motivation.

"We felt we deserved to win," Shanahan said. "We knew we were going to keep getting our chances. We didn't want to be flying across the country anymore. If we win it now, we knew we could relax and take a couple of days off."

But 20 more minutes of hockey had taken a toll. Fewer words were spoken.

There was one noticeable exception. Lapointe, who ended Game 1 a mere 59 seconds into overtime, had something to say. "There's a strong belief system in this locker room between each period," associate coach Dave Lewis said. "Our guys were saying that somebody needs to get it. Somebody do it.

"Lapointe stood up and said a few words. Marty went through it in Game 1, and he knew from experience how it felt. He was saying, 'It's a great feeling, guys. Somebody's going to get it. It's in here. Somebody's going to get it.' "

The Wings unleashed a 16-shot barrage in the second overtime and held the Ducks without a shot for 17 of the final 20 minutes.

Shanahan finally ended the affair, about five hours after it had started, and the Wings erupted in celebration. A large group congregated around him near the Ducks' goal and a smaller pack swarmed Mike Vernon (35 saves) at the opposite end.

"It's funny, because in situations like that, a lot of times everyone goes to the goal-scorer," Kris Draper said. "But Vernie was the shorter skate, so a lot of guys took advantage of that.

"We had half the guys going to Vernie and half going to Shanahan, and then everyone just sort of came together. That was a special moment."

Playing it by the numbers

Some numbing numbers from the Red Wings' marathon sweep of the Mighty Ducks, capped by a double-overtime victory at Anaheim.

3:27 a.m.
■ That's when Game 4 ended, Eastern time, probably the Wings' latest goal ever. Mud Bruneteau's six-overtime goal for a 1-0 win at Montreal in 1936 came at 2:25.

73
■ The number of shots the Wings fired at Mikhail Shtalenkov in the game. He stopped 70.

223-131
■ The Wings' edge in shots on goal in the series, including 63-35 in OT.

5⅓
■ That's how many games the sweep took in playing time, counting one hour, 19 minutes and one second of overtime in three of the games.

40:49
■ The amount of time the Wings held a lead in the series. The Ducks led for 1:06:20 and it was tied for 3:32:24.

5
■ The Wings' margin of victory (13 goals to eight). But they outscored the Ducks, 5-2, in the third period and 3-0 in overtime.

Shell-shocked Ducks goalie Mikhail Shtalenkov

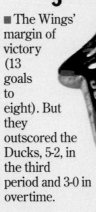

47
■ Shots Nick Lidstrom had taken in the playoffs before scoring his first goal, which tied Game 4 in the third period.

17
■ Points by the Russian Five, on six goals and 11 assists.

27.3
■ Doug Brown's shooting percentage — three goals on 11 shots.

Detroit-Anaheim: Second round
Composite Box Score

Red Wings win series, 4-0 (Home team in CAPITALS).

Date	Score	Goalies	Winning Goal
May 2, 1997	WINGS 2, Ducks 1 OT	Vernon/Hebert	Martin Lapointe
May 4, 1997	WINGS 3, Ducks 2 3OT	Vernon/Hebert, Shtalenkov	Slava Kozlov
May 6, 1997	Wings 5, DUCKS 3	Vernon/Shtalenkov	Sergei Fedorov
May 8, 1997	Wings 3, DUCKS 2 2OT	Vernon/Shtalenkov	Brendan Shanahan

Goals by period
	1st	2nd	3rd	OT	Total
Wings	2	3	5	3	13
Ducks	3	3	2	0	8

Shots by period
	1st	2nd	3rd	OT	Total
Wings	51	60	49	63	223
Ducks	35	37	24	35	131

Individual Scoring	GP	G	A	Pts.	+/-	PM	PP	S	Pct.
Sergei Fedorov	4	2	3	5	5	0	0	23	8.7
Slava Kozlov	4	3	1	4	1	2	2	25	12.0
Vlad. Konstantinov	4	0	4	4	2	6	0	11	0.0
Doug Brown	4	3	0	3	1	0	0	11	27.3
Brendan Shanahan	4	1	2	3	2	2	0	19	5.3
Steve Yzerman	4	1	2	3	1	0	0	17	5.9
Martin Lapointe	4	1	1	2	2	0	0	9	11.1
Igor Larionov	4	1	1	2	4	0	1	7	14.3
Nicklas Lidstrom	4	1	1	2	3	2	0	31	3.2
Slava Fetisov	4	0	2	2	4	14	0	8	0.0
Larry Murphy	4	0	2	2	4	0	0	19	0.0
Tomas Sandstrom	4	0	2	2	1	2	0	3	0.0
Kris Draper	4	0	1	1	E	0	0	8	0.0
Darren McCarty	4	0	1	1	E	8	0	10	0.0
Tim Taylor	1	0	0	0	-1	0	0	0	0.0
Joey Kocur	3	0	0	0	0	0	0	1	0.0
Kirk Maltby	4	0	0	0	1	2	0	11	0.0
Bob Rouse	4	0	0	0	E	6	0	6	0.0
Mike Vernon	4	0	0	0		12	0	0	0.0
Aaron Ward	4	0	0	0	-1	0	0	4	0.0

Power play: 3-19, 15.8%. **Penalty killing:** 7-11, 63.6%

Goaltending	GP	MIN	GA	Avg.	EN	SO	W	L	Shots	Save%
Mike Vernon	4	320	8	1.50	0	0	4	0	131	.939

Individual Scoring	GP	G	A	Pts.	+/-	PM	PP	S	Pct.
Paul Kariya	4	2	2	4	-4	2	2	21	9.5
Dmitri Mironov	4	0	4	4	-3	6	0	10	0.0
Teemu Selanne	4	2	0	2	-3	2	1	16	12.5
Brian Bellows	4	1	1	2	-4	2	1	15	6.7
J.J. Daigneault	4	0	2	2	-4	8	0	5	0.0
Ted Drury	3	1	0	1	E	0	0	7	14.3
Jari Kurri	4	1	0	1	-2	2	0	8	12.5
Joe Sacco	4	1	0	1	-2	2	0	5	20.0
Sean Pronger	3	0	1	1	1	0	0	3	0.0
Ken Baumgartner	4	0	1	1	1	0	0	0	0.0
Richard Park	4	0	1	1	1	0	0	4	0.0
Steve Rucchin	4	0	1	1	E	10	0	3	0.0
Warren Rychel	4	0	1	1	-1	6	0	6	0.0
Darren Van Impe	4	0	1	1	-4	4	0	9	0.0
Dave Karpa	1	0	0	0	E	2	0	1	0.0
Mike LeClerc	1	0	0	0	E	0	0	0	0.0
Kevin Todd	1	0	0	0	E	0	0	1	0.0
Jason Marshall	3	0	0	0	1	2	0	2	0.0
M. Shtalenkov	3	0	0	0		2	0	0	0.0
Bobby Dollas	4	0	0	0	-2	2	0	6	0.0
Mark Janssens	4	0	0	0	-4	6	0	6	0.0
Daniel Trebil	4	0	0	0	E	2	0	3	0.0

Power play: 4-11, 36.4%. **Penalty killing:** 16-19 84.2%

Goaltending	GP	MIN	GA	Avg.	EN	SO	W	L	Shots	Save%
Guy Hebert	2	108	3	1.67	0	0	0	1	61	.951
M. Shtalenkov	3	211	10	2.84	0	0	0	3	162	.938

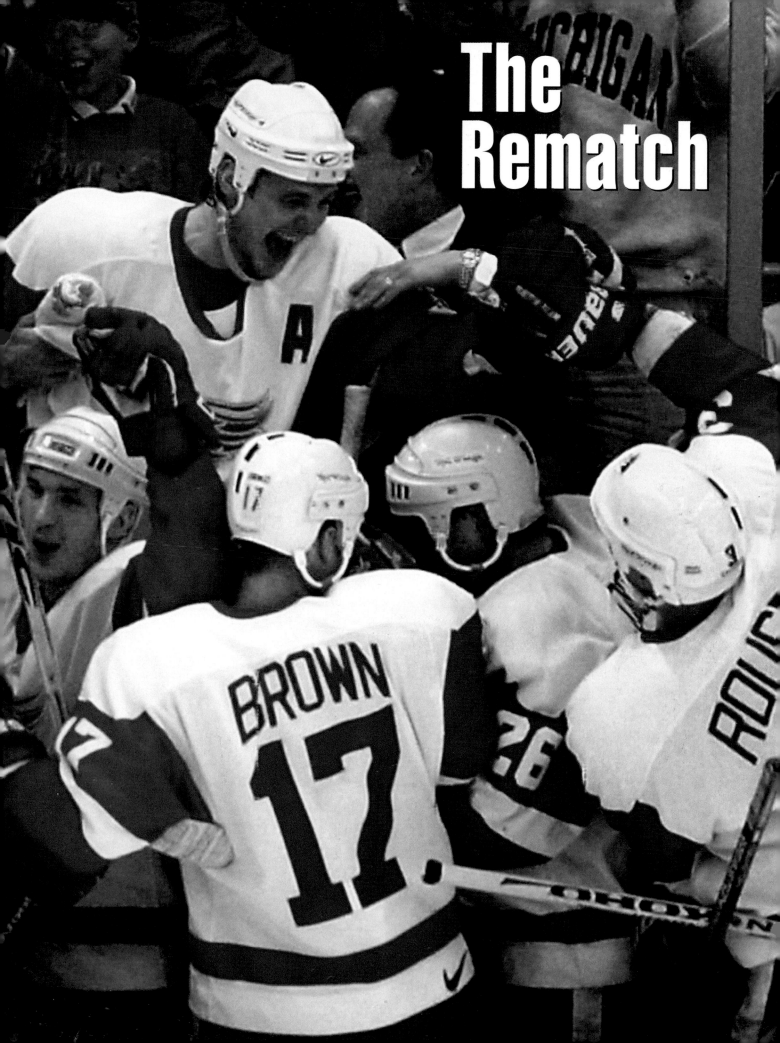

The Rematch

Time warp

Numbers don't add up, but it's still a deficit

Thursday, May 15

And so the bitter rivals met again, for the first time since the March 26 bloodbath at Detroit. This time the Wings were looking to avenge their loss in the previous year's conference finals.

By Jason La Canfora

The Red Wings outplayed Colorado for about 41 minutes Thursday night. They led the Avalanche for 27 seconds in the Western Conference finals opener. The teams were tied for another four-and-a-half minutes.

But a third-period surge by the Avalanche — just a brief display of its assembled talent — was enough to win, 2-1, at Denver's McNichols Arena.

2-1. Those are the only numbers that matter. Not the minutes. Not the seconds.

"We had a lapse in the second period, and we can't do that against this team," Brendan Shanahan said. "To not come away with a win is disappointing."

The Wings did so much right for so long. By unofficial count, they had three times as many scoring chances. They had almost twice as many shots on goal.

"We held our own and had an opportunity to win," defenseman Larry Murphy said. "That makes it hard to swallow."

The Wings finally beat Patrick Roy early in the third period when Steve Yzerman pushed the puck to Martin Lapointe, off to the side of the goal. Lapointe sent it out front, where Shanahan knocked in a one-timer.

The Avs responded immediately. Valeri Kamensky hit the post with a backhander

Martin Lapointe looks away as Colorado's Mike Ricci and Claude Lemieux celebrate the Avs' game-winning goal in the third period.

off the ensuing face-off. Then Joe Sakic beat Mike Vernon through the five-hole and tied the game 27 seconds after the Wings took the lead.

Mike Ricci, a playoff nemesis last spring, hurt the Wings again about 4 1/2 minutes later. He skated the puck up-ice and passed to Sakic, who quickly fed Lemieux, who sent the puck back across the crease just as quickly, where Ricci had

an easy tap-in.

"They're really great scoring off the rush," Yzerman said. "They're probably the best team in the league at that."

Referee Terry Gregson made it painfully clear this potentially violent confrontation was not going to get out of hand.

Gregson called everything, often leaving Wings coach Scotty Bowman shaking his head in disgust, especially when Peter Forsberg drew two Wings penalties almost simultaneously in the first period.

Forsberg showed no signs of the

concussion he suffered a week ago. He was all over the ice, setting up the Avalanche power play that scored on an amazing 38 percent of its chances over the previous seven games. It should have been deadly with the 5-on-3 advantage.

But the Wings killed it off, with help from Lemieux's minor for cross-checking Vladimir Konstantinov from behind. They killed all five Colorado power plays, but also went 0-for-6 themselves.

"We did a good job of penalty-killing, but the bad ice conditions helped," Murphy said. "It hurt both teams' power play."

The ice was soft because of power outages at the arena and worsened as the game wore on.

Bad ice or not, the Avalanche managed just two harmless shots in the second period, while the Red Wings sent 13 Roy's way.

"I don't think we played our best game in the playoffs, and the good thing is we found a way to win," Roy said. "The team deserves a lot of credit for that."

With the Wings trailing, 2-1, Sergei Fedorov stares dejectedly at the ice during a time-out late in the game.

Radio daze

About a half-hour before the start of the Western Conference finals, Red Wings radio announcers Ken Kal and Paul Woods heard a loud boom.

It went downhill from there.

The boom accompanied a generator failure at McNichols Arena and forced Woods and Kal to broadcast on a phone.

The lack of power left the hallways beneath the arena darkened. But nowhere was the failure more evident than on the ice, which was melting beneath the players' skates.

Heavy traffic areas such as in front of the benches, the goalies and in the corners were so soft, it looked as if players were skating in sand. Intermissions were lengthened by five minutes to give the ice more time to freeze, but it didn't help much.

And in a crowded booth about halfway up in the stands, Woods and Kal had to relay this via phone.

"It's like being roommates and you're on the same line," Kal said. "You keep passing the phone back and forth and hope the operator doesn't cut you off."

Kal said he had a premonition things might get ugly when he arrived at the arena. It was a dark and stormy evening in Denver after a 77-degree day.

Kal and Woods were told at game time that it would be about 40 minutes before the power could be restored.

Two hours later, the engineer was still frantically trying to figure out how to reroute the lines.

"It's one of the biggest games of the year," Kal said. "And this happens. I thought they might delay the game, but I guess because the TV power came back on, they decided to start it anyway.

"I think down the road, this is going to be one of those things you look back on and say it's one for the memories. You'll look back and say, 'Remember that time in Colorado when we had to do the game on a phone.'"

By Helene St. James

In the Nick of time

Underrated Lidstrom saves the day in Game 2

Saturday, May 17

Even a stalwart goalie such as Mike Vernon occasionally needs a little help from his friends — and defenseman Nick Lidstrom was there in Game 2.

By Jason La Canfora

One instinct, one reflex, one split-second Saturday night epitomized Red Wings defenseman Nick Lidstrom's six-year career.

And, as usually is the case with Lidstrom, his game-saving play late in the third period went almost overlooked — it happened too quickly.

Mike Vernon stopped a Colorado shot, and Eric Lacroix pounced on the rebound and shot it past him at the open net. But it didn't go in.

When his teammates and coaches reviewed the game tape, they saw Lidstrom glide through the crease behind Vernon and stop Lacroix's shot.

Nick Lidstrom

A minute later, Darren McCarty scored on a breakaway for a 4-2 Wings victory at McNichols Arena, tying the series with Colorado at one game apiece.

"What an unbelievable play," associate coach Dave Lewis said of Lidstrom's stop. "The biggest play of the series, right there. I didn't even realize what had happened, because the play kept going. Then, after the replay, we realized what had happened. We almost fell down. I was watching the video and I almost fell down."

Despite being outshot by a wide margin — the final tally was 40-17 — the Avalanche had jumped to a 2-0 lead on goals by Scott Young and Claude

Darren McCarty raises his arms in jubilation after scoring the clinching goal in the 4-2 victory that gave the Wings a 1-1 series tie.

Lemieux. But 42 seconds after Lemieux's goal at 16:09 of the second, Igor Larionov scored for the Wings.

Detroit then scored three unanswered goals in the third period — thanks to Lidstrom — by Sergei Fedorov, Steve Yzerman and McCarty.

McCarty saw Lidstrom's play from behind the goal, where he was trapped.

"I was standing back in that position," McCarty said. "You can't get there. You're too far away. You're just watching it. Then Nick just dives across, and it hits his stick. That was definitely the break we needed."

If any Wing wasn't in awe of the play, it was Lidstrom.

The hand is quicker than the Foote as Wings goalie Mike Vernon gloves Adam Foote's point-blank shot with Colorado and Detroit tied, 2-2, in the second period.

ROUND THREE
GAME TWO

"It was my guy from the face-off, so I had to make up for letting him go along the boards," Lidstrom said. "Just instinct. Just try to get in the way. Just try to get the puck out of there.

"I just reacted. I didn't really have time to think. ... I just tried to get in front of the net. I just tried to get my stick in the way."

All in a day's work for Lidstrom.

He's one of the hardest-working players in the game. He logs more minutes than any other Wings defenseman and bears enormous offensive and defensive responsibilities.

But with other Wings drawing the media attention, Lidstrom toils in relative obscurity. Vladimir Konstantinov is a Norris Trophy finalist; the Wings believe Lidstrom should be, too.

But when the lights and cameras swarm to Yzerman and Vernon after a game, you often can find Lidstrom at his locker, going about his business quietly and happily.

"He's always overlooked," McCarty said. "That's the story of his career. He's one of the most underrated players in the league. He does it all. He plays great

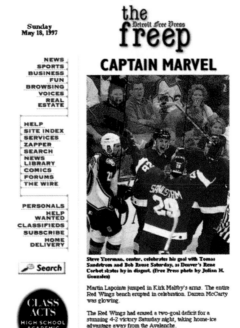

Sunday May 18, 1997

the freep

NEWS
SPORTS
BUSINESS
FUN
BROWSING
VOICES
REAL ESTATE

HELP
SITE INDEX
SERVICES
ZAPPER
SEARCH
NEWS LIBRARY
COMICS
FORUMS
THE WIRE

PERSONALS
HELP WANTED
CLASSIFIEDS
SUBSCRIBE
HOME DELIVERY

Search

CLASS ACTS
HIGH SCHOOL ACADEMIC ALL-STARS

CAPTAIN MARVEL

Steve Yzerman, center, celebrates his goal with Tomas Sandstrom and Bob Rouse Saturday, as Denver's Rene Corbet skates by in disgust. (Free Press photo by Julian H. Gonzalez)

Martin Lapointe jumped in Kirk Maltby's arms. The entire Red Wings bench erupted in celebration. Darren McCarty was glowing.

The Red Wings had erased a two-goal deficit for a stunning 4-2 victory Saturday night, taking home-ice advantage away from the Avalanche.

Full coverage

defensively. He's got a heck of a shot. He's a great offense player. He plays 35 minutes a game.

"He doesn't get the respect, but we know how good he is, and that's what counts. When your teammates appreciate you, that's all that matters."

Benched

A key member of the Red Wings sat alone in an airport hangar after Game 2 of the Western Conference finals, awaiting a return trip to Denver.

It supported three players at once during the game and drew much praise for the performance — but got stuck with a middle seat on the plane ride back to Detroit late Saturday night.

Heck, it didn't even have a name.

The mystery contributor was the small bench that a friend of associate coach Barry Smith built for the Wings.

The small, cramped visitors bench at McNichols Arena caused the Wings problems changing on the fly. Before, players had to sit on three chairs at the end of the bench, often losing their skate edges on the metal and having problems getting to the gate.

But with the extra six-and-a half-foot bench, the three overflow players could relax in comfort.

Why bring it back to Detroit?

"If we had left it in Denver, they would have burned it," trainer John Wharton said. "The arena people were not too happy about it, but the other bench wasn't working. You have to find any edge you can, and it worked great."

Wings coach Scotty Bowman had complained to the NHL about the visitors bench during the previous spring's playoffs.

"We couldn't open the gate," Bowman said. "We only had the use of one gate because we had chairs, and the chairs weren't good. It made sense to just have a bench that was portable instead of the chairs. ...

"I think it helped our game plan because we were able to get on the ice quicker. When you're on the road, you have to get your players on the ice quickly, and we did."

By Jason La Canfora

Slava Kozlov is the center of attention after one of his two goals that beat Colorado, 2-1.

Pencil them in

ROUND THREE
GAME THREE

Kozlov, Vernon do a Conn job on Avs

Monday, May 19

The Red Wings played well enough in Colorado to win both games, but came home with the series tied, 1-1 — still good enough to grab home-ice advantage.

By Jason La Canfora

Don't engrave Claude Lemieux's name on the Conn Smythe Trophy just yet. Or Patrick Roy's. "Slava Kozlov" might look better — the first Russian name to grace the maple leaf-adorned trophy as playoff MVP.

"Mike Vernon" wouldn't look bad either.

Kozlov provided the offense with two goals and Vernon stopped 27 of 28 shots Monday night as the Red Wings beat Colorado, 2-1 — and took a 2-1 lead in the Western Conference finals.

"I think he's one of our most underrated players," Darren McCarty said of Kozlov.

"He can beat you with his speed, and he can beat you with his shot. We know how important he is to the team. ..."

"He's just happy to play. He's a quiet guy. I wish I could speak Russian, because he's a really funny guy."

Kozlov's production is clear in any language. "Two times I shoot the puck, I score two goals," he said.

'Nuff said.

If there were an unsung hero award, Doug Brown would be the leading candidate. He keyed the winning goal, falling to his knees, spinning and firing the puck on goal, then springing up to screen Roy.

Fedorov won the rebound and fed Kozlov in the face-off circle. Kozlov fired high, picking the smallest of spaces above Roy's right shoulder 8:20 into the third period.

"Russians like to pass a lot, but with a shot like that, he's got to take more," defenseman Nick Lidstrom said. "The whole team has tried to tell him to take more shots."

Maybe they just needed to tell him in Russian. Kozlov and Fedorov played like stars from beginning to end.

They were the second Wings line to take the ice and netted the first goal.

About a minute into the game Fedorov beat Alexei Gusarov at the blue line and broke into the zone. He eluded Gusarov again along the boards, spun back toward the blue line and put the puck toward the goal.

Kozlov intercepted it in the slot and fired back across his body and past Roy at 1:12. The lead held up until Joe Sakic's power-play goal tied it at 14:47 of the second period.

Colorado coach Marc Crawford sent out no fewer than seven line combinations in the first seven minutes of the game, but the Avs didn't get a shot until 8½ minutes were gone.

That's when they woke up and produced 13 of the next 16 shots. And that's when Vernon did his best Roy impersonation.

"Vernon was definitely the difference,"

Adam Deadmarsh, who couldn't beat Wings goalie Mike Vernon, also finds his way blocked by Kris Draper.

defenseman Sandis Ozolinsh said. "He stopped us on the power plays."

It's true Vernon was at his best when the Wings took three penalties in a 5:32 span. The most stunning save came on Colorado's first power play when a dump-in caromed off the boards and into the slot.

Vernon was behind the goal to play the puck, but had to dash around the goal and out front to scoop up Adam Deadmarsh's weak shot at the 99 percent-open net.

"When we need him, he's there," Lapointe said.

But a goalie can do only so much, and Sakic's power-play goal tied the game late in the second period after a series of bad Wings penalties.

Kozlov made sure the Red Wings closed the game as strong as they opened it and gave playoff MVP voters something else to think about.

He and Vernon gave their team another victory — the most important thus far.

The eyes have it as infuriated Red Wings defenseman Aaron Ward comes to grips with Colorado defenseman Sylvain Lefebvre in the third period. When the final punch was thrown, each was penalized with a fighting major and a misconduct.

Bad Blood II

'Happy Trails' littered with Avs' frustrations

Thursday, May 22

It finally happened. With the Red Wings running away with the game, the bad blood between these two teams boiled over again.

By Jason La Canfora

The sound track to a series emanated through a desolate Red Wings dressing room, where sticks and helmets sat in 26 empty lockers after Thursday night's game.

The song sent a message to the Colorado Avalanche that no Wings player would.

"Happy Trails to You."

The lyrics, coming from a stereo in the training room, were a perfect summary of the Wings' 6-0 dismissal of the Avalanche in Game 4 of the Western Conference finals at Joe Louis Arena.

The Wings led the series, 3-1, and had played well enough to earn a sweep. But there was nary a laugh, much less a grin,

Avalanche captain Joe Sakic better pack a lunch: He's listening to the third-period penatiles.

Colorado's Marc Crawford lectures Detroit's Scotty Bowman, who took his coaching rival to school.

ROUND THREE
GAME FOUR

from the Wings as they spoke stoically with the media after a savage third period.

"I've got nothing to say," Darren McCarty said. "You guys watched the game. Report what you saw."

What the Wings did was humiliate the Avs on all fronts. They got two-goal games from playmaker Igor Larionov and grinder Kirk Maltby, who had three in the entire regular season.

Goalie Mike Vernon, without saying a word, outshined and silenced Colorado's Patrick Roy with his 19-save shutout — his first of this playoff.

This wasn't a win to be savored; it was a necessary war, a means to an end.

"Exactly," Wings defenseman Larry Murphy said. "There's no reason to celebrate. This game doesn't mean anything. We've got nothing, and we have to remember that."

The Wings' silence seemed more effective than the endless complaints from the Colorado players and coaches and their weak attempts to intimidate the Wings late in the game.

Play dissolved in the third. The Avalanche racked up 100 minutes in penalties and their coach, Marc Crawford, made an embarrassing attempt to get at

Crawford vs. Bowman

When the Red Wings and Avalanche say they don't like each other, they mean it.

While the players scuffled on the ice in the third period of Game 4, the coaches got in a shouting match on the bench — led by, who else, Colorado's Marc Crawford.

With 2:18 left, Crawford climbed the glass to a photographers' well that separates the benches and screamed at Scotty Bowman.

"He was pretty emotional," Bowman said. "I told him, 'It's a game, it's over, there's about two minutes left.' His eyes were coming out of his head. So he was pretty excited."

Bowman also calmly told Crawford: "I knew your father before you did, and I don't think he'd be too proud of what you're doing right now."

"Then again, maybe he would be," Bowman said of Floyd the next day, "because he's a competitor.

"His father was an ultra-competitor," said Bowman, who remembered the elder Crawford from his junior days with Belleville (Ontario). "He played a lot like (Vladimir) Konstantinov. He hated to lose, and he didn't give an

inch. The Crawfords are tough people."

As for Marc Crawford, he apologized for the incident that cost him $10,000 in fines: "I embarrassed the league, and more important I embarrassed my team. And for that, I am sorry. There's no way you can justify anything like that. If you try to, it's wrong. I was wrong."

Penalty minutemen

The infamous brawlfest March 26 might have had more blood than Game 4, but it was no match in penalty minutes. In March, the teams combined for 148 minutes; but they had 204 in just the third period Thursday, en route to 236 for the night.

Among the penalties in the final period were eight fighting majors, 10 misconducts, three game misconducts, two instigating penalties and one goalie interference, while the puck was in the neutral zone (thanks, Rene Corbet).

The bloodiest battle?

When Brendan Shanahan roughed up Corbet. Shanahan bled from friendly fire (an errant Martin Lapointe stick). Corbet, holding a towel to the back of his head, needed two people to get him to the bench.

Wings players and coaches after several minutes of screaming.

"You say some things and they say some things," Crawford said. "Things got out of hand. Nobody is proud of it."

The Avs moan. The Wings score. The Avs whine. The Wings win.

This was Detroit's game from beginning to end. The Avs were bombarded by 14 Wings shots and mustered two weak attempts of their own in the first period.

Wings coach Scotty Bowman tinkered with a sputtering power play, teaming Larionov with Slava Kozlov and Martin Lapointe, and the unit clicked 1:52 into the game.

Larionov shot across the goal and Colorado defenseman Alexei Gusarov reached back with his stick and poked the shot right between Roy's pads, exactly as Anaheim's J. J. Daigneault did on Steve Yzerman's shot in Game 2 of the second-round series.

Six more minutes of Wings dominance produced the second goal.

Brendan Shanahan's shot blasted off Jon Klemm's skate and sailed to the opposite side, where Lapointe grazed it. The loose puck went to Larionov, who fluttered a high backhander into the net.

The Avs had yet to produce a shot. In desperation, Crawford used his only time-out of the game. It didn't help. Colorado was whistled for five minor penalties in the period, giving it five more penalties than scoring chances.

The Wings were just getting started. They scored three goals in about seven minutes. Kozlov darted from the penalty box and beat Roy on a breakaway for his eighth goal in 10 games. Sergei Fedorov's one-timer from the point flew by Roy's glove hand, dinged off the post and the light came on. Maltby send Roy to the showers with his first goal, then beat backup Craig Billington.

Kirk Maltby scored the Wings' fifth and sixth goals; he practices his best Joe Louis High-Step after the final one, in the third period.

A little r evenge

Avs give Wings a taste of their own 6-0 medicine

Saturday, May 24

The Wings cruised back to Denver leading the series, 3-1, and coming off a 6-0 victory at home. But turnabout's fair play, eh?

By Jason La Canfora

What goes around, comes around. Everything the Red Wings gave Colorado in Game 4 was handed right back to them Saturday night at McNichols Arena.

Colorado staved off elimination and thrashed the Wings, 6-0. The Wings still held a 3-2 lead in the series, but realistically, Monday night's Game 6 in Detroit suddenly became a must-win for both teams.

"It was a good performance tonight, but we have to have a great performance, our best road game of the year, in Detroit," Avalanche coach Marc Crawford said. "We know that. We're well aware of it."

The shutout gave Avalanche goalie Patrick Roy three in nine home games and 11 in his career. He yielded five goals on 25 shots in two periods Thursday night but stopped all 32 in Game 5.

"I just have to give credit to the guys in

Claude Lemieux celebrates an early goal against Mike Vernon that helped set the tone of Colorado's wipeout of the Wings. Valeri Kamensky joins in.

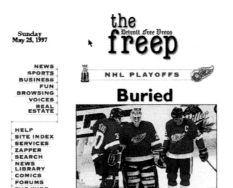

front of me," Roy said. "This was the best game we've played. We were outstanding as a team."

Joe Sakic (25 points) and Claude Lemieux (24) regained their form as well, each scoring twice to remain 1-2 in playoff scoring.

The Avalanche, playing without injured star center Peter Forsberg (charley horse), was the better team from the opening face-off.

For the first time, the Avs outhit the Wings, starting when Yves Sarault leveled Larry Murphy behind the Detroit goal. Avalanche players unanimously credited grinders Sarault and Brent Severyn with setting the tone early.

The Wings didn't dominate the neutral zone and made too many turnovers. Wings goalie Mike Vernon, often left

That really gets my goatee

It was not my place — as a man who needs a month to grow a five-o'clock shadow — to ask why Red Wings players suddenly sported the same facial hair. But I did it anyhow. Someone had to. I mean, if everyone in your office suddenly came to work looking like Magic Johnson, you'd ask, "What's going on?" Wouldn't you?

So what went on?

"I don't know," said Aaron Ward, rubbing his mustache. "I just grew mine because you're supposed to."

"Don't ask me," said Darren McCarty, scratching his beard. "I don't know who started it."

"It's a team thing," said Joe Kocur, stroking his chin. "I don't know who started it either. You just do it to be part of the group."

Well, it worked. The Wings' locker room suggested a Dennis Miller look-alike contest. A stream of Fu Manchu-meets-goatees, one right after the other. Brendan Shanahan had one. Kirk Maltby had one. Doug Brown, Chris Osgood, Kris Draper, Martin Lapointe, Tomas Holmstrom, Jamie Pushor.

Hair, there and everywhere. Even the clean-cut Swede, Nick Lidstrom, had one. At least I think he had one. It was that, or white clam sauce.

And it was not just the players. The equipment crew was semi-bearded. Same went for the support staff — right down to the masseur.

"It's a crazy superstition," admitted John Wharton, the suddenly hairy trainer. He plucked at his goatee. He looked a little like the devil. "I hate it. It feels terrible. To be honest, I never wanted to grow it."

"Then why did you?"

He laughed. "Darren McCarty threatened to shave every inch of my body hair if I didn't."

Well. It's hard to argue with that.

But here's the thing. Most of these players — while believing in the concept of "the team that gets soup in its beard together, stays together" — didn't think they looked particularly good.

MITCH ALBOM

"My wife won't even kiss me," Brown moaned.

"I had to start growing mine three weeks before the playoffs," Ward said, "otherwise I'd look like a leprechaun."

"Even my daughter asked me to shave mine off," Kocur said. "Personally, I think I look like bleep."

He glanced around the room. "Hey, we all look like bleep."

But that was the idea, right? Grunge together, win together? It was not a new concept. Playoff beards had been an NHL habit for years.

But not shaving was one thing. That at least saved you time. Keeping these Fu Manchu/goatee jobs, well, that was an effort, wasn't it? You had to shave the sides, but not the front? You had to try to keep a straight line going?

"Not me," Ward said. "I push my face with one finger and shave to the left of it, then I push it on the other side and shave to the right. There's no finesse in this beard."

Nor was there much in McCarty's curly effort. Poor Darren. He was the ultimate team guy. He would give his left arm for a teammate. But he was burdened with a light, straggly beard that only offered small tufts on his chin.

"I am not facial hair-endowed," he moaned.

To be honest, he looked like the world's first Amish hockey player.

But hey. It's not his fault. He was just standing by the new team motto: "Hair we go, boys."

Of course, not every Red Wing took part. Steve Yzerman had one going, but shaved. Most of the Russian players remained smooth-faced.

The hirsute tradition must have been a pain — especially when the players sweated. And when they rubbed their hairy chins, the Wings looked like a team of college professors pondering the next question.

But team spirit was team spirit. Good-bye, Gillette. Later, Lectric Shave. Lately, I even noticed fans coming unshaven to the games.

And if the Wings win a few Stanley Cups, who knows? This city may not shave for years.

Which means they'll have to change that song. To "Get Up, Hairytown."

Doesn't have much ring to it, does it?

without any help, was chased early in the second period.

"There wasn't one good thing to say about this team," forward Brendan Shanahan said. "Not a single player was happy with his game. It's almost appropriate we got shellacked. It's a good wake-up call."

Lemieux scored the first two goals, giving him a league-leading 13 this season and 70 in his playoff career. That broke a tie with Wings great Gordie Howe and equaled Mario Lemieux for 10th all-time.

Lemieux's first tally, at 6:46, ended Colorado's 92-minute, nine-second scoring drought. He scored again at 11:04.

Joe Sakic made it 3-0 at 15:34 of the first period, and Stephane Yelle's goal ended Vernon's night at 2:23 of the second. Vernon, who gave up four goals on 11 shots, was last pulled April 22 in Game 4 of the first-round series with St. Louis.

"At that point in time, we weren't playing well enough to pull out the win, and he's had a long stretch," Bowman said. "He's had no relief at all."

Chris Osgood made his second appearance of the playoffs in a mop-up role and gave up goals to Sakic and Scott Young before the period ended. Osgood stopped 15 of 17 shots.

"They took the attack early in the first period," Bowman said. "Obviously, we didn't have enough attack. … We didn't go after rebounds. … We didn't shoot high when we could have shot high. … We didn't screen.

"If you don't do those things, you probably come out with a shutout against you."

Dared not, and did not

After getting lost twice, they find way to a big win

Monday, May 26

Coming off their worst loss of the playoffs, the Wings came home to Joe Louis Arena with a chance to clinch the series — or face a Game 7 in Denver.

By Mitch Albom

The game was in the final minute, the Colorado goalie was pulled, and finally … finally … there really was nothing standing between the team and the dream. Brendan Shanahan raced to the loose puck, took good aim and put that baby in the open basket, unleashing a flood of noise that could be heard all the way to the Rocky Mountains.

Guess who's coming for Stanley — again? From a warm summer Saturday, two years ago, deep in the swamps of New Jersey, the Red Wings had been waiting to get back to this night. Waiting for a chance to redeem their squandered potential, to correct the road they mistakenly turned off when last they journeyed to the NHL finals.

"This team has so much character," said a sweaty but happy Mike Vernon, the goaltending hero of this series, after the Wings dethroned defending champion Colorado with a 3-1 victory that sealed the Western Conference finals, four games to two. "Now we're going to the big one."

Well. One big one at a time. Monday night was already a Game 7 disguised as Game 6. The Wings dared not blink. They did not blink. They dared not tire. They never tired. They dared not lose. And so they did not lose.

"I told the team that they would rue

Martin Lapointe scored the Wings' first goal on a shot that seemed to pass right through Colorado goalie Patrick Roy's glove.

GAME SIX

the day if they didn't show up and play the game of their lives," coach Scotty Bowman said. "You always want to remember the game that put you into the Stanley Cup finals, not the one that you didn't win to get there."

Right. The Wings had way too much of that last year. So Monday, Memorial Day, marked the death of bad memories, and all the redemption you could squeeze into

one thumping, bumping, crazy-loud hockey rink. Bye-bye, Claude Lemieux. Au revoir, Patrick Roy. See you, Joe Sakic.

Colorado was the team the Wings needed to beat to heal their own wounds. The Avs snuffed the Wings last year, left them bleeding and humbled, left Kris Draper in the hospital. The hunger for revenge simmered all season, like a giant poison stew.

Finally, that odor was gone. It began to waft in the second period, when Martin Lapointe fired a slap shot at Roy. The goalie tried to catch it, then sank in

Shaken up

There still was bad blood between Claude Lemieux and the Red Wings after the Western Conference finals-clinching victory at Joe Louis Arena.

Lemieux and Kris Draper broke with playoff postgame tradition and did not shake hands.

Ditto for Lemieux and Darren McCarty.

Lemieux shattered Draper's face with a hit from behind in the 1996 playoffs, and the Wings forward had to endure a summer of rehabilitation.

McCarty, one of Draper's best friends, got revenge against Lemieux by beating him to a bloody pulp when the teams met March 26.

During the playoff postgame handshakes, Draper refused to shake with Lemieux. Then Lemieux refused to shake hands with McCarty, who was next in line.

"Obviously there's a lot of bad blood between these two hockey clubs," Draper said. "But you look the players in the eye, and they shake your hands and you shake their hands. Some guys that don't like you a lot wish you good luck.

"I was just going through the line and I looked at him, and as soon as he saw me, he just kind of turned away and threw his hand out. So that's an indication for me just to skate by, and that's why I did it.

"If he would have looked at me. … It would have been nice if he had something to say. But obviously he didn't. He feels he doesn't have to do that. That's fine. I looked at him, he looked away and stuck his hand out. That's not sportsmanship. … That's not up to me to go grab his hand. I didn't do anything wrong."

Lemieux would say only: "That says it all, that says it all."

McCarty said he offered his hand to Lemieux in the spirit of sportsmanship only to see his efforts rejected.

"He didn't want to shake my hand," McCarty said. "I'm not going to worry about it. He's not real high on my priority list. I'm a better person than that. … I'm not going to lose any sleep over it."

By Jason La Canfora

Sergei Fedorov, who got the wind knocked out of him trying to check Colorado's Aaron Miller, scored the game-winner at 6:11 of the third period.

disbelief when it went off his glove and trickled into the net. The supposedly unbeatable Roy stared at his glove, as if there were a hole in it.

There was no hole.

Not in the glove, anyhow.

But the invincibility of Colorado was shot. The deciding nail came one period later, when Sergei Fedorov slapped one shot at Roy, then took his own rebound and poked it through. This is the same Sergei Fedorov who missed most of the first two periods because he couldn't breathe after slamming himself into an opponent for a check.

"How does it feel to beat these guys?" forward Doug Brown was asked. "Losing last year was so bitter."

"This is exactly the opposite of bitter," he said, grinning. "You find the adjective."

OK. How about sweet, delicious, satisfying, cleansing, enthralling, complete? Any of those work?

Detroit was the better team in four of the six games, some might even say five

of the six. It wasn't just the big moments — the spectacular goals, the nerve-jangling saves — it was all the moments between the big moments that won this thing.

It was every hard check, and every two-man sandwich on a speedy Colorado player. It was every puck stolen before the Avalanche could mount an attack, and every peppering attack on Roy that made him work, made him think, tired him out.

It was every fight the Wings skated away from. It was all the rushes that went unrewarded with goals, but kept the flow of the game red, red, red.

It was Vernon making the little saves, not just the big ones. It was Bowman making the right line changes. It was the endless trade imbalance on the shots-on-goal board.

And it was heroics, too. Like captain Steve Yzerman going coast-to-coast in Game 2, like Slava Kozlov doing all the scoring in Game 3, like Igor Larionov with two fast goals in Game 4, like Fedorov injuring himself, then coming back to score the killer Monday night.

It was Shanahan firing like a madman all night long, finally hitting pay dirt on the last goal of the series.

"I knew from the moment I came here they kind of got me for this series," Shanahan said. "Last year at this time, I had no idea I would be here. All I can say is thanks to this organization. And we're not finished yet."

No, they're not. Now they head for Philadelphia, another hockey town where they have waited a long time for a Stanley Cup. The Flyers are big and tough and have the league's most eagerly awaited superstar, Eric Lindros, looking to scratch his name into the Cup. And, of course, there's Paul Coffey, whose departure — in the Shanahan trade — might have been the turning point in this Detroit season.

But for now, it felt good to be rid of all that anger, frustration, jealousy, regret, bad memories, visions of Sakic shooting and Roy pumping his stick and Lemieux laughing at his destruction.

And the best way to avoid a return of those emotions was simple: Win four of the next seven games.

Yzerman accepted the Campbell Bowl on Monday night and quickly skated off with it. Two years ago, he held it over his head and enjoyed the fans' celebration, only to feel despair four games later. Looking back, he felt bad about that, as if he and his team had somehow celebrated prematurely.

Colorado goalie Patrick Roy, cocky in his comments leading up to the game, was silenced by a barrage of goals in Game 6.

"I didn't want to make a big deal out of it," he said this time.

OK. No big deal. The Wings had simply reached a plateau on this mountain, a place to take out the canteens, swig a few sips, glance around at the view, and then pack up and keep ascending. The Holy Grail was just over yonder hill.

Got the bowl. Want the Cup.

Have fun storming the castle, boys.

The Vladinator

Vladimir Konstantinov, surveying the situation at practice before the start of the Stanley Cup finals in Philadelphia, has the work ethic for getting the job done.

There's a word for him ... if we could find it

The Red Wings went into the Stanley Cup finals expecting a physical series against the Philadelphia Flyers. And that meant extra duty for defenseman Vladimir Konstantinov.

By Mitch Albom

There is a word for what he does, we just don't know what it is. Instigator? Annoyance-maker? Stick-poker? Technically, he is a defenseman, but he pretty much goes where he has to go, following the other team's best player and trying to give him fits.

Irritator? Aggravator? Head-gamer?

He has never led the league in scoring, nor in assists, nor in saves, but he is considered at the top of his craft — whatever that craft is.

Provoker? Nerve-jangler? Button-pusher?

He looks mean and he looks old, but he is neither mean nor old. He is a man with a job to do, and as the son of a fisherman from the Russian town of Murmansk, he has the work ethic for getting the job done.

"His job, I guess, is to get under other people's skin," says Joe Kocur. "To check them, hit them, get them off their game. He's intense. He's non-stop. If everyone was brought up with his mentality? The world would be at war all the time."

Well. Welcome to the bumpy world of Vladimir Konstantinov — better known as "Vladdie" to fans, or "Vlad the Impaler" to enemies.

He is not a goon in the traditional sense. He is not out there to beat people up. He draws not blood, but ire.

There is a word for this. Somewhere ...

Exasperator? Exacerbator? Elbow-in-the-facer?

"What is your job?" I ask.

Konstantinov smiles, which on his face means the cheeks move a quarter of an inch. Konstantinov, 30, is handsome enough, but in a rough way, with sharply defined bone angles and skin lines, a strong jaw, straight blondish hair. He looks like the guy who shows up in a pea coat and a black cap and works the docks on the graveyard shift.

"My job," he says, in his thick accent, "is to have strong game."

"Is there a name for what you do?"

Again he smiles. Another quarter-inch

Konstantinov and Philadelphia's Rod Brind'Amour tangle against the boards in Game One of the Stanley Cup finals in Philadelphia.

THE FINALS

cheek move. "Is not my style to talking," he says.

OK. Fine. People forget the Red Wings' Russians, as much as they have become a part of local lore, have only been in this country maybe six or seven years. They've had to learn a new language, a new league, a new style.

Well, for Konstantinov, not all that new a style.

"Were you always this kind of player?" I ask.

"No," he says. "When I am young I am a defenseman. I play regular defense. When I join Red Army, I turn."

Temper-tickler? Back-shover? Rage-monger?

"The thing about Vladdie is we all love him," Darren McCarty says. "We love him, because so few guys are willing to do what he does, but what he does is his passion."

"And what is that?"

"Beating on everyone's face."

Whatever you call whatever Konstantinov does, it would be of critical importance in the Stanley Cup finals.

Against the Philadelphia Flyers, the Wings were overmatched in the size and strength department — with the exception of Vladdie.

He gives them edge. He gives them attitude. His job would be to badger Eric Lindros, provoke him, distract him, annoy

him anyway he can, with a poke here, a shove there, anything to get him off his game.

"Remember the last time we played?" Kocur says. "Lindros wanted to take Vladdie's head off!"

Konstantinov is Bill Laimbeer on skates. (Check that. He probably can jump higher than Laimbeer, even with his equipment on.) He is annoyance personified, the kind of guy you hate on another team but love on your own.

He is not Claude Lemieux. He has more guts than Claude Lemieux. He is not Bob Probert. He is more stick and less fist than Bob Probert.

He is a man with a mission, one which he seems to understand, even if he can't always put it into words.

"Do you mind that the fans outside of Detroit don't like you?" I ask.

"It's good they don't like me," he says. "They not supposed to like me."

There's a video they show at Joe Louis Arena which inter-cuts scenes from "The Terminator" with shots of Konstantinov crashing into opponents: "He can't be stopped! ... He feels no pain! ... He feels no remorse!"

At the end, Vladdie is shown wearing sunglasses, with his arms folded. He says, "Hasta la vista, baby."

Hmm. A Russian, speaking Spanish, in a mostly Canadian sport, played in America. You know what that means?

It means have fun, Philadelphia. He's all your problem now.

Wings beat 'em like a drum

Flyers are supposed to be physical, but they get caught in the grind

Saturday, May 31, 1997

The Red Wings went to Philadelphia looking to do something they hadn't for 31 years — win a game in the finals.

By Jason La Canfora

Speed beat size. Almost everything beat Philadelphia goalie Ron Hextall. And, lately, nothing beats the Red Wings.

The Wings silenced a thunderous crowd at the CoreStates Center on Saturday night and whacked the Flyers, 4-2, in Game 1 of the Stanley Cup finals.

The Wings hadn't won a game in the finals since a 5-2 victory over Montreal on April 26, 1966.

"I am not overly excited with it," Steve Yzerman said. "It is a good start to the series, but it is just getting under way, and winning the first game isn't necessarily an indication of the way the series is going to go."

But some trends were apparent. The Flyers' five-game home winning streak was over, and all of their weaknesses were exposed.

An older, thin defense turned the puck over considerably and helped the Wings take a lead they never lost. And Hextall, who began the playoffs as a backup, broke his team's back with about 19 minutes to play.

The Wings took a 3-2 lead into the third period, but the Flyers had scored late in the second and came out flying, primed for a comeback.

Then Yzerman wheeled through the neutral zone, got one skate across the blue line and fired, just for the heck of it, from 60 feet. Hextall tried a kick save, and the puck beat him five-hole — an unforgivable error that couldn't have come at a worse time.

"I could have knocked nine pucks into the corner," said Yzerman, who beat

Flyers goalie Ron Hextall felt the heat in Game One. Coach Terry Murray would get him out of the kitchen for Game Two.

St. Louis' Grant Fuhr in the first round with a 90-footer. "I didn't."

Yzerman wasn't the only Wing to surprise. Detroit had three breakaways in the first period — by sniper Brendan Shanahan and the Grind Line's Kirk Maltby and Joe Kocur. Guess which two buried their chances?

Maltby, a recent Sports Illustrated cover boy, disproved the SI jinx moments after Shanahan was stuffed. Eric Lindros misplayed the puck trying to enter the Detroit zone, and Maltby broke in alone with Kris Draper.

Maltby dished to Draper in front of the goal, and Hextall dashed to cover him. Draper returned the favor to Maltby, who fired into the vacant right side of the net for a shorthanded goal just 6:38 into the series.

On the next shift, with the Flyers still on the power play, Lindros hacked at goalie Mike Vernon while he was stopping Janne Niinimaa's shot. Nick Lidstrom couldn't tie up the 6-foot-4, 236-pound Lindros, and Rod Brind'Amour poked in the rebound. The Wings' lead had lasted 59 seconds.

The Flyers went on the offensive for the next five minutes. The Wings had trouble clearing the zone, especially on rebounds in front of Vernon, and seemed content to ice the puck on numerous occasions. They went more than nine minutes without a shot.

Another grinder would change that. Kocur, playing in the over-30 "beer leagues" a few months earlier, intercepted Kjell Samuelsson's clearing attempt and waltzed in on Hextall.

Kocur went hard to his forehand, and Hextall bit on the fake, pulling to the right post. Kocur roofed his backhander, and the Wings took a 2-1 lead into the second period.

"In practice I try that move all the time and the puck usually ends up in the corner by the boards," Kocur said.

Clockwise from lower left, Kris Draper, Steve Yzerman, Sergei Fedorov and Martin Lapointe congratulate goalie Mike Vernon on another job well done.

Grinders in full gear: Kris Draper, left, and Kirk Maltby are exuberant after Maltby's fourth goal of the playoffs opened the finals scoring.

The Flyers were the aggressors again at the start of the second period, but the Wings survived an early flurry and the Wings returned to setting the tempo.

Sergei Fedorov won a face-off in the Detroit end, and got it back on the rush through the neutral zone.

Larry Murphy jumped in for a two-on-one, but this was Fedorov's play all the way. He held the puck and unleashed a wrist shot that beat Hextall high to his glove side for a 3-1 lead.

With just under three minutes left in the second period and four seconds after Philadelphia's fifth power play expired, Mikael Renberg cut up-ice, split the defense and opened a huge hole on the left wing for John LeClair.

Renberg passed to LeClair, forcing Vernon to slide cross-crease, and LeClair fired right between his pads, cutting the lead to 3-2.

But thanks to Yzerman's goal and another solid period by Vernon, the final 20 minutes belonged to Detroit, as it did throughout the playoffs.

GAME 1 SUMMARY
Red Wings 4, Flyers 2

Detroit	2	1	1 — 4
Philadelphia	1	1	0 — 2

First period
Detroit, Maltby 4 (Draper), 6:38 (sh)
Phila., Brind'Amour 11 (Lindros, Niinimaa), 7:37 (pp)
Detroit, Kocur 1, 15:56

Second period
Detroit, Fedorov 6 (Murphy, McCarty), 11:41
Philadelphia, LeClair 8 (Renberg, Lindros), 17:11

Third period
Detroit, Yzerman 5 (Murphy), :56

Penalties
1st: Sandstrom, Det (high-sticking), 5:50; Fetisov, Det (interference), 11:26; Klatt, Phi (interference), 17:09; Kocur, Det (interference), 19:42. **2nd:** Lacroix, Phi (interference), 5:48; Fedorov, Det (tripping), 7:08; Fetisov, Det (interference), 15:07; Klatt, Phi (charging), 17:45. **3rd:** Svoboda, Phi (crosschecking), 6:27; Lindros, Phi (roughing), 17:48.

Shots: Detroit 8-12-10—30; Philadelphia 10-9-9—28. **Power plays:** Detroit 0 of 5; Philadelphia 1 of 5. **Goalies:** Detroit, Vernon (13-4); Philadelphia, Hextall (4-1). **A:** 20,291. **Referee:** Bill McCreary. **Linesmen:** Ray Scapinello, Dan Schachte.

Philadelphia's Petr Svoboda takes a flier, courtesy of Wings enforcer Darren McCarty.

Full game coverage in Sports

Kirk Maltby continued his hard hitting on the Flyers and Chris Therien,
but it was Maltby's winning shot in the second period that made him the hero of Game 2.

Snowed under

Kirk Maltby's game-winner buries the Flyers

Tuesday, June 3, 1997

A lot of teams would be satisfied to open with a split on the road. But after winning Game 1 at Philadelphia, the Red Wings were primed to grind out another victory.

By Jason La Canfora

He raises his arms, flashes a surprised smile and calmly skates over to the Red Wings' bench. He has just scored the go-ahead goal and changed the tenor of the Stanley Cup finals with one slap shot.

Just another day in the life of Kirk Maltby, grinder-turned-playoff star. Maltby scored one of the biggest goals in recent franchise history, the winner in Tuesday's 4-2 victory over the Flyers, but he was as laid-back and aw-shucks as ever after the game.

"The whole thing has been what you dream about as a kid," Maltby said. "I'm just happy to be here."

The Wings, who decided between taking Maltby or a 12th-round draft pick in a 1996 trade with Edmonton, were happy he was here, too. They took a dominating 2-0 lead in the finals, thanks in large part to Maltby.

Maltby watched the Wings blow a two-goal lead in the final 2:18 of the first period. He sat helplessly on the bench as the Flyers outskated and outhit the Wings, rejuvenated the Core-States Center crowd, and renewed their own Stanley Cup hopes.

Then Maltby did something about it. He churned along the right wing and blasted a shot from about 45 feet, above the face-off circle, and beat goalie Garth Snow low to the glove side.

"I didn't even see it go in," Maltby said.
The Wings led, 3-2, and the Flyers

New goalie, same result. Philadelphia's Garth Snow replaced Ron Hextall between the pipes in Game 2, but the Wings beat him, too, 4-2.

were deflated. Brendan Shanahan one-timed a pass from Martin Lapointe with 9:56 left for his eighth goal of the playoffs. 4-2. Game over.

What a week. Maltby scored goals in four of the past five games — including both finals games — appeared on the cover of Sports Illustrated and shattered the so-called SI jinx.

"As far as the SI cover, that was just a fluke," Maltby said. "It was being in the right place at the right time."

This was the same Kirk Maltby who

went 36 games before scoring this season. The same Kirk Maltby who played 21 career playoff games before scoring this spring. The same Kirk Maltby with six goals in the past two seasons combined.

"I played against Malts in junior, and he scored 50-some goals," Darren McCarty said. "He can put the puck in the net."

Maltby provided the perfect ending to an unbelievable beginning to Game 2. The Wings orchestrated the ideal scenario in the opening minutes but returned to the dressing room a much more somber group.

The game opened with another Kjell Samuelsson blunder. The defenseman's errant pass gift-wrapped Joe Kocur's breakaway goal in Game 1, and Tuesday night he lost the puck to Shanahan in the neutral zone.

Shanahan fired from about 35 feet out, off Paul Coffey's skate and past Snow on his glove side.

Coffey continued his rough series. He was on the ice for four of the Red Wings' first five goals in the series, and his second penalty of the opening eight minutes led to their second goal of the first period.

McCarty's beautiful drop pass let the Wings set up in the Flyers' zone on the man advantage. They rotated the puck to captain Steve Yzerman, who put in his own rebound from the side of the net with bangers McCarty and Tomas Sandstrom in front. The Wings led, 2-0.

Then Shanahan was sprung on a breakaway by a 55-foot pass and with an array of dekes, had Snow cleanly beaten. Fire up the motorcade. Get out the confetti. The Cup was coming back to Detroit.

Not so fast.

Instead of creating a 3-0 lead, Shanahan's shot trickled off the outside of the net with four minutes left in the

Pranks a lot

The playoffs were a frustrating time for Chris Osgood. Unfortunately for Jamie Pushor, Ozzie took it out on him.

Osgood, the anointed Red Wings goalie of the future, sat on the backup stool while Mike Vernon played brilliantly through the playoffs.

Last season, Osgood and Vernon won the Jennings Trophy for best goals-against average in the league, and Osgood began this season as the Wings' No. 1 goalie.

But come playoff time, coach Scotty Bowman — who brought Vernon to Detroit — went with experience. Osgood's only appearances came in mop-up roles.

"You want to play so badly it eats you up for a while," said Osgood, 24.

"It's a lot easier to take because we went to the finals. I'd rather be here practicing than not be here at all. It's just hard not playing.

"But it's the same as with other stuff. I try to learn from everything and make the best of the situation. You have to keep your head up."

Actually, that's the policy his teammates take with Osgood.

Head up, eyes open.

"Christopher?" good friend Pushor said. "He spends way too much time playing pranks. You have to keep your eyes on him."

Pushor held up a new pair of tennis shoes as proof: "Look at this. This is what Chris does. He's written all over my shoes.

"Here's 'Canes forever' because that's the team I played for in juniors. 'Lawyers rule.' I'm not really sure what that means.

"You know what else he does in his spare time? He packs stuff for you. We got home from Philadelphia, I unpacked my bag, and there's newspapers everywhere.

"He thinks that's funny. It's not really funny, it's just annoying."

By Helene St. James

Philadelphia fans such as Steve Thompson of Lebanon, Pa., could barely watch as the Flyers failed to win even one game at home against the Red Wings.

Goalie Mike Vernon continued his stellar play, shutting down John LeClair and the Flyers' Legion of Doom. Vernon faced 31 shots, allowing only two goals in Game 2.

period. Then the Wings fell into a defensive shell, just like Game 1, and were outshot, 13-2, for the rest of the period.

The Flyers' Rod Brind'Amour scored power-play goals 1:09 apart to tie the game before the period ended.

"They really took it to us pretty good," Larry Murphy said. "A couple of bounces and it could have been a different story."

The goals were identical. Brind'Amour won face-offs in the Wings' zone, got the puck back to rookie Janne Niinimaa, and went to the goal to deflect his shot from the point past Mike Vernon (29 saves).

That set the stage for Maltby, the playoff hero, the hockey Cinderella.

He's just happy to be here.

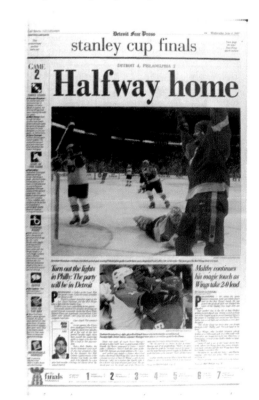

GAME 2 SUMMARY
Red Wings 4, Flyers 2

Detroit	2	1	1 — 4
Philadelphia	2	0	0 — 2

First period
Detroit, Shanahan 7, 1:37
Detroit, Yzerman 6 (Murphy, Fetisov),
9:22 (pp)
Philadelphia, Brind'Amour 12 (Niinimaa),
17:42 (pp)
Phila., Brind'Amour 13 (Niinimaa, LeClair),
18:51 (pp)
Second period
Detroit, Maltby 5 (Kocur), 2:39
Third period
Detroit, Shanahan 8 (Lapointe, Fedorov),
9:56
Penalties
1st: Coffey, Phi (holding), 4:29; Coffey, Phi
(holding), 7:24; Lapointe, Det (charging),
10:21; Fetisov, Det (high-sticking), 17:09;
Larionov, Det (holding), 18:37. **2nd:** Maltby,
Det (roughing), 6:54; Coffey, Phi (roughing),
6:54; Detroit bench, served by Brown (too
many men), 9:03; LeClair, Phi (elbowing),
12:13. **3rd:** Lapointe, Det (roughing),
10:27; Dykhuis, Phi (roughing), 10:27.

Shots: Detroit 14-9-5—28; Philadelphia 14-
9-8—31. **Power plays:** Detroit 1 of 3;
Philadelphia 2 of 4. **Goalies:** Detroit, Vernon
(14-4); Philadelphia, Snow (8-4). **A:** 20,159.
Referee: Terry Gregson. **Linesmen:** Wayne
Bonney, Gord Broseker.

**Former Wing Paul Coffey
must have wondered
how much worse it could
get as Detroit's Brendan
Shanahan and
Martin Lapointe
celebrated Shanahan's
second goal of Game 2.
Shanny's first goal
went off Coffey's skate,
and Coffey sustained a
mild concussion and
was a no-show the
rest of the series.
The Wings headed home
with a 2-0 lead.**

Captain within one win of his dream

Red Wings make Flyers' first lead of series dissolve in a 6-1 rout

Borrowing a move from pro wrestling, Darren McCarty performs a pile-driver, with Janne Niinimaa as the pile.

Thursday, June 5, 1997

Mission accomplished with two victories at Philadelphia, the Red Wings returned to the friendly confines of Joe Louis Arena.

By Jason La Canfora

Steve Yzerman stood motionless at the blue line while a packed Joe Louis Arena saluted him for a full 15 seconds. His name hadn't even been announced. It didn't have to be.

"Ste-vie! Ste-vie! Ste-vie!"

"It really gets your heart pumping," Yzerman said. "It gave me the chills. … It's a special feeling."

He is Detroit. The Red Wings are his team. This was his moment. This was their year.

The Wings were closer than ever to the Stanley Cup they have sought for 42 years after Thursday night's 6-1 thrashing of Philadelphia.

They were one game from turning a dream into reality for their captain, the guy who blocks shots with a five-goal lead and five minutes to play, the guy brought to Detroit in 1983 when the team had few fans.

"When he raised his stick to the fans … that's what it's all about," associate coach Dave Lewis said of Yzerman's attempt to quell the cheers. "That's the bond between this city and Steve Yzerman."

Thursday night, 19,983 fans never let up.

"It's crazy — it's a good crazy, not in a bad way," Darren McCarty said. "It's been dubbed Hockeytown. … You can see why."

Yzerman and his teammates made them go wild for three periods.

Sergei Fedorov continued his marvelous spring as well, scoring twice and assisting on two others. Martin

Brendan Shanahan bowls Philadelphia goalie Ron Hextall over after assisting on Sergei Fedorov's second goal of the game, on a power play at 3:12 of the second period. Shanahan scored late in the period, bouncing the puck in off Hextall.

Sergei's sterling night

Sergei Fedorov rushes to celebrate Martin Lapointe's first goal of the game, on which Fedorov assisted. Fedorov had two goals and two assists.

GAME 3 SUMMARY
Red Wings 6, Flyers 1

Philadelphia	1	0	0 —	1
Detroit	3	2	1 —	6

First period
Phila, LeClair 9 (Desjardins, Brind'Amour), 7:03 (pp)
Detroit, Yzerman 7 (Kozlov), 9:03 (pp)
Detroit, Fedorov 7, 11:05
Detroit, Lapointe 3 (Brown, Fedorov), 19:00

Second period
Detroit, Fedorov 8 (Kozlov, Shanahan), 3:12 (pp)
Detroit, Shanahan 9 (McCarty), 19:17

Third period
Detroit, Lapointe 4 (Fedorov, Vernon), 1:08 (pp)

Penalties
1st: McCarty, Det (interference), 6:10; Desjardins, Phi (holding), 8:44; Fetisov, Det (slashing), 12:14; Sandstrom, Det (holding), 12:54; Lapointe, Det (tripping), 16:43. **2nd:** Klatt, Phi (tripping), 2:24; Petit, Phi (holding stick), 10:14. **3rd:** Lindros, Phi (cross-checking), :46; Lindros, Phi (elbowing), 8:12; McCarty, Det (interference), 8:39; Fetisov, Det (slashing), 13:02; Brown, Det (slashing), 19:41.

Shots: Philadelphia 8-7-7—22; Detroit 10-12-7—29. **Power plays:** Philadelphia 1 of 7; Detroit 3 of 5. **Goalies:** Philadelphia, Hextall (4-2); Detroit, Vernon (15-4). **A:** 19,983. **Referee:** Kerry Fraser. **Linesmen:** Ray Scapinello, Dan Schachte.

You could spend all morning talking about the Red Wings' superb effort in the 6-1 victory over Philadelphia. But a special word here for Sergei Fedorov, who scored his first goal of the night on a stolen puck, a sprint and a shot right through a flailing Ron Hextall.

It was vintage Sergei, done by himself, with opposing players gasping for air and reading his number from behind.

His second score was another gem. Slava Kozlov moved in on Hextall, closer, closer, untouched, then fired a breathing-distance shot. It ricocheted off the goalie's stick, came out top to Fedorov, who rifled it past him for the big red light.

"Sometimes people think I am not trying because I am not in corners all the time," Fedorov said a few days earlier. "But maybe best way for me to help team is to watch and wait, then, at the very right moment, get like red-hot metal."

He did that Thursday night. He played hard and fast and was all over the ice. Let's face it. He has been doing that the latter half of the postseason.

His two-goal, two-assist night in Game 3 of the Stanley Cup finals was the best of any Wing during the playoffs and gave him eight goals and a team-leading 20 points — after going scoreless in the first four games.

"A great playoff," admitted the usually reserved Scotty Bowman.

Fedorov has so much pure talent that you simply cannot discount him, even if you haven't noticed him for a while.

His speed was impossible for the Flyers to defend, and his quickness made him a demon on defense.

He rose to the top when he was needed the most. And after a forgettable regular season that included stints as a fourth-line center and defenseman — he scored 63 points, 44 fewer than last season — it was good timing for him personally.

He and the Wings delayed contract negotiations until after the playoffs, when Fedorov also had the option of becoming a restricted free agent.

"Are you saving your best for last?" Fedorov was asked after the game.

"Yep," he said, in his best American.

Give the man his due. He has carried his load.

By Mitch Albom

Lapointe also scored twice. Goalie Mike Vernon was solid, making 21 saves and adding an assist.

For the first time in the series, Vernon yielded the opening goal when John LeClair put in a rebound on the power play 7:03 into the game.

But the Flyers' first lead of the finals didn't last. The rest of the evening belonged to the Red Wings.

Fittingly, Yzerman scored first. Two minutes after the Flyers took the lead, Yzerman took it away with a blistering power-play slap shot.

"Ste-vie! Ste-vie! Ste-vie!"

The crowd erupted, the bond between player and fan never stronger.

"That was a special moment for all of us," Brendan Shanahan said.

Entire sections of fans seemed to have "Yzerman 19" on their backs, from a guy wearing a Peterborough Petes sweater (Yzerman's junior team), to kids in T-shirts. There was little doubt the agony of 1995, when the Wings were swept by New Jersey in the finals and Yzerman was limited to one point, burned within their hero.

Yzerman had goals in the first three games of the finals after scoring four in the previous three rounds.

"He's done it all for us," coach Scotty Bowman said.

Yzerman assured a victory in Game 1 by stealing the Flyers' momentum in the third period with a 60-foot slap shot for a two-goal lead. In Game 2 he gave the Wings another two-goal cushion, and Thursday night he sent the message that his team would not be denied.

Then he passed the torch to Fedorov.

Fedorov burst into the zone, took the puck off Karl Dykhuis' stick as he was falling down, shook off Joel Otto's check and beat goalie Ron Hextall, back in the Flyers' net after Garth Snow's failure in Game 2.

Yzerman and Fedorov did it on defense, too, helping shut down the Flyers

Detroit goalie Mike Vernon makes one of his 21 saves in Game 3. He also scored an assist — on Martin Lapointe's second goal.

It was a rough night for Ron Hextall, especially after the Wings scored their sixth goal barely a minute into the third period.

A former Mike Vernon antagonist admits his error. Vernon yielded a goal that gave the Flyers their first lead of the series, but it didn't last.

GAME THREE   **89**

during a five-on-three power play for 1:20, with Yzerman diving to smack the puck out of the zone.

"Ste-vie! Ste-vie! Ste-vie!"

Lapointe, enjoying his finest playoff, flattened the Flyers with one minute left in the first period.

First, he leapt from the penalty box and took the puck on a breakaway, but hit the post. Larry Murphy and Fedorov kept the rebound in the zone and Doug Brown flipped the puck to the slot from behind the goal, where Lapointe finished it. The Wings led, 3-1.

As the horn blew to end the period, Yzerman was alone near center ice. Another salute.

"Ste-vie! Ste-vie! Ste-vie!"

A roar let out again 3:12 into the second when Fedorov stuffed home Slava Kozlov's rebound, and with 43 seconds left in the period, Shanahan scored from behind the goal by bouncing it in off Hextall.

Lapointe burned Hextall for the final time early in the third period and the rout was almost complete.

One final chant remained.

"Ste-vie! Ste-vie! Ste-vie!
"Sweep! Sweep! Sweep!"

Philadelphia captain Eric Lindros has reason to hang his head. He was in the penalty box twice in the third period — including when the Wings scored their sixth goal of the game. Lindros wound up with as many shots (two) as penalties.

The fans in the stands spell out their desires as the Red Wings moved within one victory of the Stanley Cup.

Detroit captain Steve Yzerman has reason to smile after Game 3. The Red Wings' faithful had given him a rousing ovation, and he gave the Wings their first goal in the 6-1 rout.

Brendan Shanahan is ready to party as the Red Wings make a beeline for
goalie Mike Vernon after their Stanley Cup-clinching victory.

Finally: The Big Prize

After 42 years,
the Cup comes home
to Hockeytown

Saturday, June 7, 1997

With a commanding 3-0 lead over Philadelphia, the Red Wings had a chance to win the series at home and deliver fans their first Stanley Cup since 1955.

By Jason La Canfora

The future Hall of Famer emerged from Joe Louis Arena about 3:15 Sunday morning, carrying the one thing he had waited all his life to earn.

Steve Yzerman, the Red Wings' captain for 11 years, strutted out of the dressing room with the Stanley Cup held above his head, walked into the players' parking lot, placed the Cup in the backseat, jumped in his Porsche, and drove off as a handful of fans roared outside.

Two generations have passed since a Red Wing hoisted the Cup, kissed it, paraded it around the ice and handed it off to his teammates and coaches. Yzerman's departure brought to a close one of the wildest nights in Detroit's history, one of the biggest parties in 42 years — the last time the Wings had won the Cup.

"I don't know how to describe the way I feel," he said. "I'm glad the game is over, but I wish it never ended.

"Sometimes you hold your dream way out there and wonder if you can ever be as good as your dream. It was almost like I wanted to sit back and watch it all and not miss a minute of it."

There was so much to savor. The memories will last a lifetime. The score of Game 4 of the Stanley Cup finals, 2-1, might be forgotten. The goal-scorers, Nick Lidstrom and Darren McCarty — he of the Cup-clincher — could get lost in the telling of this tale to future generations.

But the images of celebration will never die. That's why battered and weary men hurl themselves in front of speeding pucks and shrug off sticks to the face. That's why they play the game.

This night belonged to the Wings and their fans.

The frustration was finally lifted at 10:50 Saturday night. The Philadelphia Flyers were defeated, the horn blew, the pounds of confetti fell to the ice, the fireworks went off — startling Wings coach Scotty Bowman, already wearing his Stanley Cup champions cap.

Helmets, gloves, sticks and pads were sent skyward and scattered all over the ice. The bench emptied and a mass of Red Wings engulfed goalie Mike Vernon, the Conn Smythe winner as playoffs MVP.

Slowly, the Wings lined up to shake

Yes! Darren McCarty just beat the Flyers' defense and goalie Ron Hextall for the Cup-clinching goal.

hands with the Flyers. "Oh, What a Night" blared from the loudspeakers and a deafening roar continued from the 19,983 standing fans. A red carpet was rolled out; Yzerman hopped it, skated over to the Wings' bench and embraced owner Mike Ilitch.

Bowman reappeared from the dressing room in his practice gear and skates. Vernon was presented with the Conn Smythe Trophy, and at 11 p.m. Yzerman touched the Cup for the first time, raising it above his head.

Yzerman wasn't sure what to do next. He asked Bowman — celebrating his seventh Cup as a coach, second-most in history — for advice. Bowman sent Yzerman off on his counterclockwise trip around the rink and made sure the rest of the team stayed behind.

This was the moment the captain had waited for since he was drafted by the Wings fourth overall in 1983. It was worth the wait.

Yzerman skated back to the bench and gave the Cup to Ilitch, who held it high. Then Yzerman passed the Cup to Slava Fetisov and Igor Larionov, who carried the trophy around the ice together, waving to fans.

"I was surprised," said Larionov, 36. "I play with Slava for many, many years, and we wait for this for long time. It was an honor to carry the Cup after Steve Yzerman. It was great feeling in front of 20,000 people in Joe Louis Arena and people all over the world. We were talking about it was our last chance to win the Cup."

They spoke to each other in their native tongue.

"I have a lot to say to him," said Fetisov, 39. "I say to Igor, 'We have to get the Cup together.' I have been through so many years and lots of hockey games, lots of minutes. I can't describe it. I never forget this moment the rest of my life."

Their victory lap left an indelible mark on Slava Kozlov, who idolized the stars as a child growing up in Larionov's hometown of Voskresensk.

"I was so happy for them," Kozlov said. "They have great hockey career and now win Stanley Cup. Now they can retire. I am so happy for them. They deserve it. They should have it second after Stevie."

Bowman was next: "They said, 'You go next.' I said, I'd rather wait, and they said no. Sometimes you have to listen to the players."

Most coaches, dressed in suit and tie,

Sergei Fedorov leaps to get in on the biggest group hug ever seen on the Joe Louis Arena ice. Mike Vernon is somewhere in the middle of it.

hold the Cup briefly, then pass it on. Not Bowman. Not this time.

"I always wanted to be a player in the NHL and skate with the Cup," he said. "How many chances do you get to do that? I said if we win, I'll go for it. I have always dreamt about doing that."

Vernon was a little worried about the weight of the trophy and Bowman's age, 63. "I just hoped that when they gave it to him, he didn't fall with it and dent the Cup so I couldn't drink out of it," he said.

Bowman's brother Jack, a scout with Buffalo, was surprised by the scene.

"I was glad to see him on the ice with his skates on, getting around," Jack Bowman said. "He enjoyed it. He was like a kid out there. That's the first coach I've ever seen after the game out there with his skates on, which I thought was a nice touch."

The Cup made its way to Brendan Shanahan, Sergei Fedorov, Larry Murphy and the rest of the team. The training and coaching staffs held it. Even Al Sobotka, the Joe Louis employee famous for swinging octopi above his head, got to lift the Cup.

Doug Brown had his eldest son, Patrick, on his shoulder and his daughter Anna nearby.

"That was really special," Brown said. "That just adds to it. They've come home from school for three years now during the playoffs singing the song all the little kids sing, 'We want Stanley, we want the Cup.'

"Tell me that doesn't put pressure on you, when you've got a 5-year-old little boy telling you, "We want Stanley, we want the Cup.' "

Then they skated a final victory lap as

Darren McCarty climbs the penalty box to give the fans a special salute.

a team, Yzerman in the lead, taking two minutes to circle the ice. They plopped down at center ice for a team picture, Yzerman closest to the Cup, and at 11:15 the party shifted to the dressing room, where hundreds of family members and friends awaited.

Joe Kocur, rescued from an over 30 beer league by the Wings, cracked open a beer mysteriously given to him before Game 1 of the finals. Someone placed it in his locker before he arrived at the CoreStates Center in Philadelphia, and Kocur kept it.

Saturday night, Kocur went right for the Bud Light and drank it warm with fellow Grind Liners Kirk Maltby and Kris Draper. On this night, their time alone as a team was minimal.

"There wasn't much time to have any individual talks," Maltby said. "We just came in here and mayhem pretty much broke out. We still have a few days here. The boys will get a chance to talk to each other and congratulate and get things into perspective."

Kocur already had things in perspective.

"Coming up with this team and growing up with Stevie, it's very special," Kocur said. "Where I was in mid-December, basically out of hockey, being here right now is unbelievable.

"When we won the Cup in New York, I was injured and didn't play that game, so I just wanted to skate to the corner where my mom and dad were and hoist it in front of them.

"All they went through and what they did for me when I was young, having to drive 40 or 50 miles to get to the game, those are the things you remember. That's why it means so much."

The dressing room was packed with journalists and well-wishers, including Kocur's parents. The pungent aroma of cigars, sweat and champagne was so intense it made nostrils burn and eyes water. Compact discs by Pearl Jam and U2 played throughout the night.

Families took turns taking pictures with the Cup in the weight room. Fans with their bodies painted somehow managed to get by security and thanked their heroes for bringing home the trophy.

Steve Yzerman hoists the Cup with Red Wings owner Mike Ilitch.

Slava Fetisov, left, and Igor Larionov have shared a lot over the years, and now the Stanley Cup.

GAME 4 SUMMARY
Red Wings 2, Flyers 1

Philadelphia	0	0	1 — 1
Detroit	1	1	0 — 2

First period
Detroit, Lidstrom 2 (Maltby), 19:27

Second period
Detroit, McCarty 3 (Sandstrom, Yzerman), 3:02

Third period
Philadelphia, Lindros 12 (Desjardins), 19:45

Penalties
1st: LeClair, Phi (holding), 3:23; Larionov, Det (interference), 4:31; Lindros, Phi (interference), 9:22; Falloon, Phi (holding stick), 13:21. **2nd:** Konstantinov, Det (interference), 9:27. **3rd:** Samuelsson, Phi (slashing), 1:32; Podein, Phi (high-sticking), 11:54; Draper, Det (slashing), 14:39.

Shots: Philadelphia 8-12-8—28; Detroit 9-10-8—27. **Power plays:** Philadelphia 0 of 3; Detroit 0 of 5. **Goalies:** Philadelphia, Hextall (4-3); Detroit, Vernon (16-4). **A:** 19,983. **Referee:** Bill McCreary. **Linesmen:** Wayne Bonney, Gord Broseker.

"You see all the people around here, they give us so much support," said Fedorov, who played with broken ribs. "I never thought we have so many friends and so many fans that can support us.

"I'm telling you, I've been drinking champagne all night long, that's how I feel right now. It's great. Do we have any more champagne around here? No more champagne?"

This was a game the players had been planning for all their lives. They opened their eyes Saturday morning knowing this could be the day to deliver a city from a curse and make their dreams come true.

"I woke up this morning, and I was a bag of nerves," said Murphy, who won his third Cup. "I'm so excited it ended. When you've won the Cup before, you know how exciting it is and you try to keep it quiet and low-key, and it was tough. I had to keep it under wraps.

"I don't think anyone realized what this was going to be like. And I've seen it before and I didn't want to tell anybody because I think it would have been a distraction. It was a test. The last few days were a test."

For two days, Detroit had been proclaiming them champions, from song parodies on the radio to signs all over the city. When players arrived at the Joe around 5 p.m., the streets and parking lots were lined with fans.

"It was great just driving into the game today, to see the fans," Lidstrom said. "They were out there on the streets cheering you on. It's unbelievable for the city."

Maltby said: "It was crazy. I've never seen anything like that before. I've never seen that kind of traffic and people in the streets. I've never seen so many jerseys. It's just awesome. This city deserves this, we deserve this and it's just a great feeling all around."

Before the game, Yzerman spoke up, like he did after a crushing loss in the fourth game of the first-round playoff series against St. Louis, like he did in Game 3 of the finals.

"He said, 'Let's make sure we come out hard and we do our job,' " Martin Lapointe said. " 'We're professionals. It doesn't matter what we did in the past, it only matters what we do tonight. We've got to play the game of our lives.' "

Brendan Shanahan got what he came to Hockeytown for: a chance to lift the Cup.

The Cup even brought a big smile to the normally stoic Scotty Bowman's face as he toted it around the rink.

But the captain didn't want his team uptight. Just before the players took the ice, he began a game of movie trivia with Shanahan, a fellow film buff, changing the mood in the room.

"You don't have to get up for a game like this, you have to stay loose," Shanahan said. "So before the game, he started throwing some movie names out there, and the whole team kind of looked at him. We needed to relax.

"He threw 'Tootsie' at me. Come on, 'Tootsie'? It was on TV this afternoon. I caught the last 10 minutes before I came to the rink. I said, come on, don't waste my time."

They were loose, but lucky to have a one-goal lead after one period. The Flyers were outplaying Detroit for the first time in the series, but Lidstrom's goal with 32.8 seconds left made it 1-0.

Kocur asked the coaches to leave the dressing room between periods, and addressed his teammates. It was time to get serious and realize what was at stake.

"What he said was true, and I think he'd been waiting to say it for a long time," McCarty said. "He said everybody in this room will end up in different places over the course of their life. The one thing that will keep us together will be this. You're fired up as it is, but definitely, it really puts things into perspective. It was phenomenal."

Kocur was speaking from experience, calling on the Cup he won with the Rangers three years ago.

"We'll always have each other," Kocur said of his teammates. "We'll always have tonight. This is the moment that the city, this team and everyone in this organization has always wanted to be a part of, and no one can ever take it away.

"We're all from different places in the world and we're all going to different places in the world, but from what we just did here tonight, we're all going to be together in our hearts forever. This is something nobody in this room, as long as they live, will ever forget."

McCarty scored a beautiful goal to give the Wings a 2-0 lead in the second, dropping defenseman Janne Niinimaa to the ice with a brilliant move, coaxing goalie Ron Hextall out of the crease with another, and depositing the puck into the empty side of the net.

The goal exemplified the entire spring. Another player came forward, an unexpected hero, and contributed in the clutch. No one player had to shoulder the

Most years the Red Wings' dreams have gone up in smoke. This time Darren McCarty puffed on a victory cigar.

Mike Vernon, the Conn Smythe Trophy winner as playoff MVP, takes a big gulp from the Stanley Cup.

burden of victory. It was everyone's responsibility.

"Probably in the final run, the Draper-Maltby-Kocur line gave us the final ingredient," Bowman said. "They let the star players know they could count on anybody."

After McCarty's goal, everyone in the building knew what would take place that night. With about five minutes remaining, the Black Aces, players regularly scratched from playoff games, descended from the press box into the dressing room.

They were going to greet their teammates on the ice in full equipment and participate in the skating of the Cup. Even goalie Kevin Hodson threw on his pads to join the fun.

"I said, 'I'm not playing, but I'm not going out there in a suit. I'm putting my stuff on,' " said Tim Taylor, veteran leader of the Aces. "So that's what we did. We all decided it. I made my own decision. These guys did what they wanted to do, and they followed.

"All of the guys were happy to see us when we got out there. They thought it was pretty cool. It was nerve-racking. It was five minutes left when we got dressed, and we had a penalty and our hearts sank, but here we are."

They are champions in a city that was so desperate for one.

"It's a great city, and all the players love playing here," Bob Rouse said. "If you're stuck in some city that doesn't have that history, it's just not the same. Ted Lindsay is around the dressing room all the time.

"You can feel the history on an everyday basis. It was brought up quite a few times, how long it's been."

It will be brought up no longer. The Red Wings will return to Joe Louis Arena for training camp this fall as defending champions. They will get their rings and watch the banner raised to the rafters. They will be cheered, deified, immortalized.

For now, they all can bask in the glow of their accomplishments. The Red Wings played with a sole purpose and unwavering commitment.

The Cup is theirs.

"What a story," Murphy said, nursing a beer while still in full uniform and equipment at 2 a.m., three hours after the game. "This team got better as we went along.

"By the end, no one could touch us.

"No one.

"Convincing champions."

Caution: Stanley Cup on board. Steve Yzerman left the Joe with the prize in the backseat of his Porsche.

Detroit-Philadelphia: The Finals
Composite Box Score

Detroit wins, 4-0 (home team in CAPITALS)

Date	Score	Goalies	Winning Goal
May 31, 1997	Wings 4, FLYERS 2	Vernon/Hextall	Sergei Fedorov
June 3, 1997	Wings 4, FLYERS 2	Vernon/Snow	Kirk Maltby
June 5, 1997	WINGS 6, Flyers 1	Vernon/Hextall	Sergei Fedorov
June 7, 1997	WINGS 2, Flyers 1	Vernon/Hextall	Darren McCarty

Goals by Period

	1st	2nd	3rd	OT	Total
Flyers	4	1	1	0	6
Red Wings	8	5	3	0	16

Shots by Period

	1st	2nd	3rd	OT	Total
Flyers	40	37	31	0	108
Red Wings	41	43	31	0	115

Individual Scoring

Individual Scoring	GP	G	A	Pts.	+/-	PM	PP	S	Pct.
Sergei Fedorov	4	3	3	6	2	2	1	16	18.8
Brendan Shanahan	4	3	1	4	3	0	0	13	23.1
Steve Yzerman	4	3	1	4	3	0	2	12	25.0
Martin Lapointe	4	2	1	3	3	6	1	7	28.6
Larry Murphy	4	0	3	3	10	0	0	6	0.0
Kirk Maltby	4	2	1	3	2	2	0	8	25.0
Darren McCarty	4	1	2	3	4	4	0	6	16.7
Joey Kocur	4	1	1	2	3	2	0	6	16.7
Slava Fetisov	4	0	2	2	E	10	0	5	0.0
Slava Kozlov	4	0	2	2	1	0	0	4	0.0
Nicklas Lidstrom	4	1	0	1	6	0	0	14	7.1
Doug Brown	4	0	1	1	1	2	0	3	0.0
Kris Draper	4	0	1	1	3	2	0	4	0.0
Tomas Sandstrom	4	0	1	1	2	4	0	5	0.0
Mike Vernon	4	0	1	1		0	0	0	0.0
Vlad. Konstantinov	4	0	0	0	-1	2	0	3	0.0
Igor Larionov	4	0	0	0	2	4	0	1	0.0
Bob Rouse	4	0	0	0	3	0	0	2	0.0
Aaron Ward	4	0	0	0	1	0	0	0	0.0

Power Play: 4-18 — 22.2% **Penalty Killing:** 15-19 — 78.9%

Goaltending

Goaltending	GP	MIN	GA	Avg.	EN	SO	W	L	Shots	Save%
Mike Vernon	4	241	6	1.50	0	1	4	0	108	.944

Individual Scoring

Individual Scoring	GP	G	A	Pts.	+/-	PM	PP	S	Pct.
Rod Brind'Amour	4	3	1	4	E	0	3	10	30.0
John LeClair	4	2	1	3	-5	4	1	14	14.3
Eric Lindros	4	1	2	3	-5	8	0	12	8.3
Janne Niinimaa	4	0	3	3	-4	0	0	10	0.0
Eric Desjardins	4	0	2	2	-1	2	0	9	0.0
Mikael Renberg	4	0	1	1	-2	0	0	4	0.0
Dan Kordic	1	0	0	0	E	0	0	0	0.0
Daniel Lacroix	2	0	0	0	E	2	0	1	0.0
Michel Petit	2	0	0	0	-1	2	0	1	0.0
Petr Svoboda	1	0	0	0	E	2	0	0	0.0
Paul Coffey	2	0	0	0	-5	6	0	2	0.0
Karl Dykhuis	3	0	0	0	-3	2	0	3	0.0
Pat Falloon	3	0	0	0	-1	2	0	4	0.0
Colin Forbes	3	0	0	0	-1	0	0	3	0.0
John Druce	4	0	0	0	E	0	0	3	0.0
Dale Hawerchuk	3	0	0	0	-3	0	0	2	0.0
Trent Klatt	4	0	0	0	-3	6	0	2	0.0
Joel Otto	4	0	0	0	-3	0	0	4	0.0
Shjon Podein	4	0	0	0	-3	2	0	11	0.0
Kjell Samuelsson	4	0	0	0	-3	2	0	4	0.0
Chris Therien	4	0	0	0	-2	0	0	5	0.0
Dainius Zubrus	4	0	0	0	-4	0	0	4	0.0

Power Play: 4-19 — 21.1% **Penalty Killing:** 14-18 — 77.8%

Goaltending

Goaltending	GP	MIN	GA	Avg.	EN	SO	W	L	Shots	Save%
Ron Hextall	3	178	12	4.05	0	0	0	3	87	.862
Garth Snow	1	58	4	4.14	0	0	0	1	28	.857

Mike Vernon dives across the crease to stop a shot by Philadelphia's Trent Klatt. In 20 playoff games, Vernon had a 16-4 record and a 1.76 goals-against average.

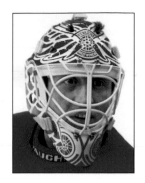

Vernon: The man behind the mask

With his second Cup, goalie redeemed himself

By Helene St. James

Surrounded by his teammates, Mike Vernon heard his name announced as the winner of the Conn Smythe Trophy, the most valuable player in the playoffs.

So he politely skated over, picked up the trophy from commissioner Gary Bettman — and held it for all of about 10 seconds. He couldn't set it down fast enough.

"I wanted to get rid of it," a champagne-soaked Vernon said later. "I wanted to get Lord Stanley out there, because that's what we're all here for. The Conn Smythe is a nice little gesture, but it takes a team effort, and everybody is deserving of it.

"The Stanley Cup was what we all wanted to hold up. That was truly a great feeling."

For two years, one thought had festered in the veteran goaltender's mind.

Redemption.

He had to find a way to get the Red Wings back to the Stanley Cup finals before his time in Detroit ran out.

And this time, win the Cup.

Vernon accomplished all that when the Wings swept Philadelphia in the finals and erased memories of 1995, when they were swept by New Jersey.

As Vernon skated around the Joe Louis Arena ice with the Cup, fans who once booed him serenaded him with chants of "Ver-nie! Ver-nie!"

"That was truly a great feeling," he said.

And a satisfying one.

Vernon, 34, was the Wings' first major acquisition after Scotty Bowman became player personnel director.

He was acquired for defenseman Steve Chiasson in June 1994 from Calgary,

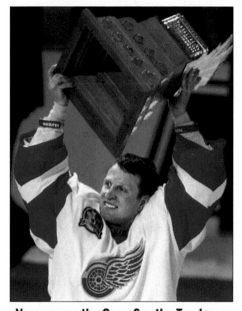

Vernon won the Conn Smythe Trophy as most valuable player of the playoffs. But he cut short his parade of the Smythe so he could hoist the Stanley Cup itself.

where he had won a Cup in 1989. Vernon's mission was to bring stability and experience to the much-maligned Detroit goaltending job while Chris Osgood developed.

Vernon played in 30 regular-season games in his first season and helped the Wings to the finals. Last season, he and Osgood combined to win the Jennings Trophy for the lowest team goals-against average.

Vernon took on more of a backup role this season, playing in 33 games and finishing with a 2.43 goals-against average.

As the playoffs loomed, Bowman turned more to Vernon, who started six of the last 10 regular-season games. And when the playoffs began, Vernon was his man.

Twenty games later, he was 16-4 with a 1.76 goals-against average and his second Stanley Cup. He faced down some

impressive goalies, including Patrick Roy and Grant Fuhr.

"I can honestly say that this one has a lot more emotion to it," Vernon said. "The first time winning a Cup is truly an amazing feat, and I don't think I really sat back and enjoyed it. It was just craziness.

"I think this one here, with what I've gone through in the last couple years — the disappointment against Jersey and not playing that much last year — having the opportunity to capitalize on this season is truly amazing."

While Vernon refused to gloat over his Conn Smythe effort, his teammates were quite willing to do it for him.

"Nobody could be happier for Vernie," Kris Draper said. "He deserves it all the way."

"Vernie's played great for us," Darren McCarty said. "He truly deserves it."

It's amazing that Vernon stayed in Detroit long enough to have a chance at redemption.

In the summer of '95, the Wings won an arbitration case against him and he was declared a free agent. But just when it seemed they would part, the Wings signed him again.

This season, with Osgood's star on the rise, Vernon seemed expendable, perhaps as trade fodder for the help on defense the Wings said they needed.

But Vernon was not traded, and he earned a one-year contract extension through next season by fulfilling a bonus cause in his contract: The Wings won the Cup, and he had at least three victories in the finals.

Once again, it was questionable whether the Wings would keep and pay both goaltenders, and Osgood was still deemed their goalie of the future.

If this were to be Vernon's last season in Detroit, he would leave redeemed and revered.

"I'm glad I had the opportunity to prove myself," he said. "I'm glad I had the opportunity to sip from the Cup again."

Game by game

REGULAR SEASON

G	DATE	OPP.	SCORE	REC.	GOALIE	WIN/TYING GOAL
1	Oct. 5, 1996	at New Jersey	L, 3-1	0-1-0	Osgood	Thomas
2	Oct. 9, 1996	Edmonton	W, 2-0	1-1-0	Osgood	Kozlov
3	Oct. 11, 1996	Calgary	L, 2-1	1-2-0	Osgood	Reichel
4	Oct. 12, 1996	at Buffalo	W, 6-1	2-2-0	Vernon	Yzerman
5	Oct. 15, 1996	at Dallas	L, 3-1	2-3-0	Vernon	Zubov
6	Oct. 17, 1996	at Chicago	L, 2-1	2-4-0	Osgood	Chelios
7	Oct. 19, 1996	NY Islanders	W, 4-2	3-4-0	Vernon	Fetisov
8	Oct. 21, 1996	Los Angeles	W, 3-0	4-4-0	Osgood	Shanahan
9	Oct. 23, 1996	Dallas	W, 4-1	5-4-0	Osgood	Draper
10	Oct. 25, 1996	Chicago	T, 2-2	5-4-1	Hodson	Shanahan
11	Oct. 26, 1996	at Boston	W, 2-1	6-4-1	Osgood	Shanahan
12	Oct. 30, 1996	Montreal	W, 5-3	7-4-1	Osgood	Fedorov
13	Nov. 1, 1996	at Ottawa	T, 2-2	7-4-2	Osgood	Daigle
14	Nov. 2, 1996	at Toronto	L, 6-2	7-5-2	Vernon	Schneider
15	Nov. 4, 1996	Hartford	W, 5-1	8-5-2	Osgood	Fedorov
16	Nov. 6, 1996	New Jersey	L, 2-0	8-6-2	Osgood	MacLean
17	Nov. 8, 1996	at Hartford	W, 4-1	9-6-2	Vernon	Lapointe
18	Nov. 10, 1996	Tampa Bay	W, 4-2	10-6-2	Osgood	Kozlov
19	Nov. 13, 1996	Colorado	L, 4-1	10-7-2	Osgood	Forsberg
20	Nov. 15, 1996	San Jose	W, 5-1	11-7-2	Vernon	McCarty
21	Nov. 18, 1996	at Phoenix	T, 2-2	11-7-3	Osgood	McCarty
22	Nov. 21, 1996	at San Jose	W, 6-1	12-7-3	Vernon	Lidstrom
23	Nov. 23, 1996	at Los Angeles	W, 6-0	13-7-3	Osgood	Yzerman
24	Nov. 24, 1996	at Anaheim	L, 3-1	13-8-3	Vernon	Valk
25	Nov. 27, 1996	Toronto	W, 5-2	14-8-3	Osgood	Shanahan
26	Dec. 1, 1996	Florida	L, 4-2	14-9-3	Osgood	Skrudland
27	Dec. 3, 1996	Vancouver	T, 2-2	14-9-4	Osgood	Shanahan
28	Dec. 4, 1996	at Washington	W, 2-0	15-9-4	Hodson	McCarty
29	Dec. 10, 1996	Edmonton	T, 0-0	15-9-5	Osgood	
30	Dec. 12, 1996	Chicago	W, 6-2	16-9-5	Osgood	Larionov
31	Dec. 15, 1996	Toronto	W, 3-1	17-9-5	Osgood	McCarty
32	Dec. 17, 1996	at Colorado	L, 4-3	17-10-5	Vernon	Lacroix
33	Dec. 18, 1996	at Calgary	T, 3-3	17-10-6	Osgood	Simpson
34	Dec. 20, 1996	at Vancouver	L, 3-2	17-11-6	Hodson	Gelinas
35	Dec. 22, 1996	at Edmonton	W, 6-2	18-11-6	Osgood	Kozlov
36	Dec. 26, 1996	Washington	W, 5-4 (OT)	19-11-6	Osgood	Fedorov
37	Dec. 28, 1996	at NY Islanders	W, 7-1	20-11-6	Vernon	Kozlov

38	Dec. 30, 1996	Phoenix	L, 5-3	20-12-6	Osgood	Ronning
39	Jan. 3, 1997	Dallas	L, 2-1	20-13-6	Vernon	Modano
40	Jan. 5, 1997	at Chicago	T, 5-5	20-13-7	Vernon	Suter
41	Jan. 8, 1997	at Dallas	L, 6-3	20-14-7	Osgood	Harvey
42	Jan. 9, 1997	at Phoenix	W, 5-4 (OT)	21-14-7	Osgood	Larionov
43	Jan. 11, 1997	Chicago	L, 3-1	21-15-7	Osgood	Probert
44	Jan. 14, 1997	Los Angeles	T, 3-3	21-15-8	Osgood	Stevens
45	Jan. 20, 1997	at Montreal	L, 4-1	21-16-8	Vernon	Tucker
46	Jan. 22, 1997	Philadelphia	T, 2-2	21-16-9	Vernon	LeClair
47	Jan. 25, 1997	at Philadelphia	W, 4-1	22-16-9	Vernon	Shanahan
48	Jan. 29, 1997	Phoenix	L, 3-0	22-17-9	Vernon	Shannon
49	Feb. 1, 1997	at St. Louis	W, 4-1	23-17-9	Vernon	Shanahan
50	Feb. 2, 1997	Dallas	W, 4-3 (OT)	24-17-9	Osgood	Kozlov
51	Feb. 4, 1997	St. Louis	T, 1-1	24-17-10	Vernon	Campbell
52	Feb. 6, 1997	Vancouver	L, 7-4	24-18-10	Osgood	Gelinas
53	Feb. 8, 1997	at Pittsburgh	W, 6-5 (OT)	25-18-10	Vernon	Shanahan
54	Feb. 12, 1997	San Jose	W, 7-1	26-18-10	Osgood	Shanahan
55	Feb. 14, 1997	at Dallas	L, 4-3 (OT)	26-19-10	Vernon	Kennedy
56	Feb. 16, 1997	at Florida	W, 4-2	27-19-10	Osgood	McCarty
57	Feb. 17, 1997	at Tampa Bay	T, 3-3	27-19-11	Vernon	Langkow
58	Feb. 19, 1997	Calgary	W, 4-0	28-19-11	Osgood	Sandstrom
59	Feb. 22, 1997	at St. Louis	T, 2-2	28-19-12	Vernon	Turgeon
60	Feb. 24, 1997	at Phoenix	W, 5-3	29-19-12	Osgood	Kozlov
61	Feb. 27, 1997	Pittsburgh	W, 4-1	30-19-12	Vernon	Fedorov
62	March 1, 1997	NY Rangers	W, 3-0	31-19-12	Osgood	McCarty
63	March 2, 1997	Anaheim	T, 1-1	31-19-13	Vernon	Drury
64	March 5, 1997	at Toronto	T, 4-4	31-19-14	Osgood	Sundin
65	March 8, 1997	at Vancouver	W, 5-3	32-19-14	Vernon	Larionov
66	March 10, 1997	at Los Angeles	T, 3-3	32-19-15	Osgood	Ferraro
67	March 12, 1997	at Anaheim	L, 2-1	32-20-15	Vernon	Kurri
68	March 15, 1997	at San Jose	W, 7-4	33-20-15	Osgood	Kocur
69	March 16, 1997	at Colorado	L, 4-2	33-21-15	Osgood	Jones
70	March 19, 1997	Boston	W, 4-1	34-21-15	Hodson	Larionov
71	March 21, 1997	at NY Rangers	L, 3-1	34-22-15	Osgood	Courtnall
72	March 23, 1997	at Chicago	L, 5-3	34-23-15	Hodson/Vernon	Krivokrasov
73	March 26, 1997	Colorado	W, 6-5 (OT)	35-23-15	Vernon	McCarty
74	March 28, 1997	Buffalo	W, 2-1 (OT)	36-23-15	Vernon	Murphy
75	March 30, 1997	Anaheim	L, 1-0 (OT)	36-24-15	Vernon	Rucchin
76	April 1, 1997	St. Louis	T, 1-1	36-24-16	Vernon	Taylor
77	April 3, 1997	Toronto	T, 2-2	36-24-17	Osgood	Taylor
78	April 5, 1997	at Toronto	W, 4-2	37-24-17	Osgood	Yzerman
79	April 8, 1997	at Calgary	W, 3-2 (OT)	38-24-17	Osgood	Sandstrom
80	April 9, 1997	at Edmonton	T, 3-3	38-24-18	Vernon	Sandstrom
81	April 11, 1997	Ottawa	L, 3-2	38-25-18	Vernon	Redden
82	April 13, 1997	St. Louis	L, 3-1	38-26-18	Osgood	Demitra

WESTERN CONFERENCE: FIRST ROUND

G	DATE	OPP.	SCORE	SERIES	GOALIE	WINNING GOAL
1	April 16, 1997	St. Louis	L, 2-0	0-1	Vernon	Courtnall
2	April 18, 1997	St. Louis	W, 2-1	1-1	Vernon	Murphy
3	April 20, 1997	at St. Louis	W, 3-2	2-1	Vernon	Yzerman
4	April 22, 1997	at St. Louis	L, 4-0	2-2	Vernon	Courtnall
5	April 25, 1997	St. Louis	W, 5-2	3-2	Vernon	McCarty
6	April 27, 1997	at St. Louis	W, 3-1	4-2	Vernon	Shanahan

WESTERN CONFERENCE: SECOND ROUND

G	DATE	OPP.	SCORE	SERIES	GOALIE	WINNING GOAL
1	May 2, 1997	Anaheim	W, 2-1 (OT)	1-0	Vernon	Lapointe
2	May 4, 1997	Anaheim	W, 3-2 (3 OT)	2-0	Vernon	Kozlov
3	May 6, 1997	at Anaheim	W, 5-3	3-0	Vernon	Fedorov
4	May 8, 1997	at Anaheim	W, 3-2 (2 OT)	4-0	Vernon	Shanahan

WESTERN CONFERENCE FINALS

G	DATE	OPP.	SCORE	SERIES	GOALIE	WINNING GOAL
1	May 15, 1997	at Colorado	L, 2-1	0-1	Vernon	Ricci
2	May 17, 1997	at Colorado	W, 4-2	1-1	Vernon	Yzerman
3	May 19, 1997	Colorado	W, 2-1	2-1	Vernon	Kozlov
4	May 22, 1997	Colorado	W, 6-0	3-1	Vernon	Larionov
5	May 24, 1997	at Colorado	L, 6-0	3-2	Vernon	Lemieux
6	May 26, 1997	Colorado	W, 3-1	4-2	Vernon	Fedorov

STANLEY CUP FINALS

G	DATE	OPP.	SCORE	SERIES	GOALIE	WINNING GOAL
1	May 31, 1997	at Philadelphia	W, 4-2	1-0	Vernon	Fedorov
2	June 3, 1997	at Philadelphia	W, 4-2	2-0	Vernon	Maltby
3	June 5, 1997	Philadelphia	W, 6-1	3-0	Vernon	Fedorov
4	June 7, 1997	Philadelphia	W, 2-1	4-0	Vernon	McCarty

WINGS' REGULAR-SEASON STATS

PLAYER	GP	G	A	PTS	+/-	PM	PP	SH	GW	SHT
Shanahan	81	47	41	88	32	129	22	3	7	336
Yzerman	81	22	63	85	22	78	8	0	3	232
Fedorov	74	30	33	63	29	30	9	2	4	273
Lidstrom	79	15	42	57	11	30	8	0	1	214
Larionov	64	12	42	54	31	26	2	1	4	95
McCarty	68	19	30	49	14	126	5	0	6	171
Kozlov	75	23	23	46	21	46	3	0	6	211
Murphy	81	9	36	45	3	20	5	0	1	158
Sandstrom	74	18	24	42	6	69	1	2	2	139
Konstantinov	77	5	33	38	38	151	0	0	0	141
Lapointe	78	16	17	33	-14	167	5	1	1	149
Fetisov	64	5	23	28	26	76	0	0	1	95
Draper	76	8	5	13	-11	73	1	0	1	85
Rouse	70	4	9	13	8	58	0	2	0	70
Brown	49	6	6	12	-3	8	1	0	0	69
Dandenault	65	3	9	12	-10	28	0	0	0	81
Pushor	75	4	7	11	1	129	0	0	0	63
Holmstrom	47	6	3	9	-10	33	3	0	0	53
Maltby	66	3	5	8	3	75	0	0	0	62
Taylor	44	3	4	7	-6	52	0	1	0	44
Ward	49	2	5	7	-9	52	0	0	0	40
Eriksson	23	0	6	6	5	10	0	0	0	27
Kocur	34	2	1	3	-7	70	0	0	1	38
Osgood	46	0	2	2	0	6	0	0	0	0
Knuble	9	1	0	1	-1	0	0	0	0	10
Hodson	6	0	1	1	0	0	0	0	0	0
Vernon	33	0	0	0	0	35	0	0	0	0

+/- — plus-minus rating (a plus is added for being on the ice when a goal is scored for a player's team in a full-strength situation; a minus is added for being on the ice when an opponent's goal is scored in a full-strength situation); PM — penalty minutes; PP — power play goals; SH — shorthanded goals; GW — game-winning goals; SHT — shots on goal.

GOALIES	GP	MIN	AVG	W-L-T	SO	GA	SH	SV%
Hodson	6	294	1.63	2-2-1	1	8	114	.930
Osgood	47	2769	2.29	23-13-9	6	106	1175	.910
Vernon	33	1952	2.43	13-11-8	0	79	782	.899
Team	**82**	**5031**	**2.35**	**38-26-18**	**7**	**197**	**2075**	**.905**

WINGS' PLAYOFF STATS

PLAYER	GP	G	A	PTS	+/-	PM	PP	SH	GW	OT	SHT
Fedorov	20	8	12	20	5	12	3	0	4	0	79
Shanahan	20	9	8	17	8	43	4	0	2	1	82
Kozlov	20	8	5	13	3	14	4	0	2	1	58
Yzerman	20	7	6	13	3	4	3	0	2	0	65
Larionov	20	4	8	12	8	8	3	0	1	0	29
Lapointe	20	4	8	12	8	60	1	0	1	1	37
Murphy	20	2	9	11	16	8	1	0	1	0	51
Lidstrom	20	2	6	8	12	2	0	0	0	0	79
Maltby	20	5	2	7	6	24	0	1	1	0	35
McCarty	20	3	4	7	1	34	0	0	2	0	34
Brown	14	3	3	6	4	2	0	0	0	0	23
Draper	20	2	4	6	5	12	0	1	0	0	30
Kocur	19	1	3	4	5	22	0	0	0	0	16
Fetisov	20	0	4	4	2	42	0	0	0	0	27
Sandstrom	20	0	4	4	-3	24	0	0	0	0	36
Konstantinov	20	0	4	4	-1	29	0	0	0	0	29
Pushor	5	0	1	1	-1	5	0	0	0	0	3
Vernon	20	0	1	1	0	12	0	0	0	0	0
Holmstrom	1	0	0	0	-1	0	0	0	0	0	0
Taylor	2	0	0	0	-1	0	0	0	0	0	0
Osgood	2	0	0	0	0	2	0	0	0	0	0
Ward	19	0	0	0	1	17	0	0	0	0	9
Rouse	20	0	0	0	8	55	0	0	0	0	14

GOALIES	GP	MIN	AVG	W-L	SO	GA	SH	SV%
Vernon	20	1229	1.76	16-4	1	36	494	.927
Osgood	2	47	2.55	0-0	0	2	21	.905
Team	**20**	**1280**	**1.78**	**16-4**	**1**	**38**	**515**	**.926**

1996-97 NHL STANDINGS

WESTERN CONFERENCE
CENTRAL

	W	L	T	PTS	GP	LST 10	GF-GA	AWAY
2x-Dallas	48	26	8	104	82	5-3-2	252-198	23-13-5
3y-**Detroit**	38	26	18	94	82	4-3-3	253-197	18-14-9
5y-Phoenix	38	37	7	83	82	5-3-2	240-243	23-18-0
6y-St. Louis	36	35	11	83	82	5-3-2	236-239	19-15-7
8y-Chicago	34	35	13	81	82	6-3-1	223-210	18-14-9
Toronto	30	44	8	68	82	4-4-2	230-273	12-24-4

PACIFIC

	W	L	T	PTS	GP	LST 10	GF-GA	AWAY
1xz-Colorado	49	24	9	107	82	4-6-0	277-205	23-14-4
4y-Anaheim	36	33	13	85	82	6-2-2	245-233	13-21-7
7y-Edmonton	36	37	9	81	82	3-5-2	252-247	15-21-5
Vancouver	35	40	7	77	82	6-1-3	257-273	15-23-3
Calgary	32	41	9	73	82	2-7-1	214-239	11-23-7
Los Angeles	28	43	11	67	82	3-5-2	214-268	10-28-4
San Jose	27	47	8	62	82	3-6-1	211-278	13-24-4

EASTERN CONFERENCE
ATLANTIC

	W	L	T	PTS	GP	LST 10	GF-GA	AWAY
1xz-New Jersey	45	23	14	104	82	6-3-1	231-182	22-14-5
3y-Philadelphia	45	24	13	103	82	5-3-2	274-217	22-12-7
4y-Florida	35	28	19	89	82	3-4-3	221-201	14-16-11
5y-NY Rangers	38	34	10	86	82	5-4-1	258-231	17-20-4
Washington	33	40	9	75	82	5-4-1	214-231	14-23-4
Tampa Bay	32	40	10	74	82	4-3-3	217-247	17-22-2
NY Islanders	29	41	12	70	82	4-5-1	240-250	10-23-8

NORTHEAST

	W	L	T	PTS	GP	LST 10	GF-GA	AWAY
2x-Buffalo	40	30	12	92	82	2-7-1	237-208	16-19-6
6y-Pittsburgh	38	36	8	84	82	4-5-1	285-280	13-25-3
7y-Ottawa	31	36	15	77	82	7-3-0	226-234	16-19-7
8y-Montreal	31	36	15	77	82	5-4-1	249-276	14-19-8
Hartford	32	39	11	75	82	5-4-1	226-256	8-24-8
Boston	26	47	9	61	82	2-8-0	234-300	12-27-2

x-division winner; y-playoff berth; z-conference title

Photographers

■ **Karin Anderson:** 1B. ■ **Andrew Cutraro:** 18.
■ **Kirthmon F. Dozier:** 24, 25.
■ **Steve Dykes:** 5. ■ **Kim Kim Foster:** 26.
■ **Julian H. Gonzalez:** 6, 8, 13, 14, 15, 16, 17, 20, 21, 28, 29T, 29C, 30, 33, 34, 37, 39, 59, 60, 63, 65, 67, 68, 71, 75, 86, 89T, 89R, 97, 98, 107.
■ **Bill Janscha:** 10. ■ **J. Kyle Keener:** 54R.
■ **Tom Pidgeon:** 29. ■ **Gene J. Puskar:** 22, 23.
■ **Mary Schroeder:** 7, 9, 32, 38, 40, 42, 43, 44, 45, 47, 48, 51B, 52, 53, 54L, 56, 61, 62, 66B, 69, 72, 76, 77, 79, 80, 81, 82, 87, 88, 90T, 96, 99, 102, 104, Gabriel B. Tait: 2R, 11, 35, 36, 50, 51T, 64, 66T, 73, 78, 83, 84, 85, 89L, 90B, 91, 100, 101, 106.
■ **Nico Toutenhoofd:** 2L, 49, 92, 94, 95.

KEY: T—top; C—center; B—bottom; R—right; L—left.

Detroit's **7** Degrees of Separation from our **1997** CUP

The Red Wings' latest Stanley Cup is their eighth — more than any other U.S.-based franchise.

■ **1936:** The Wings swept the Maroons, then beat Toronto, 3-1, in the best-of-five finals. Game 1 against Montreal was the longest ever, a 1-0 win ending on Mud Bruneteau's goal at 16:30 of the sixth overtime. Pete Kelly scored the Cup-winning goal, 3-2.

■ **1937:** Larry Aurie tied for the league lead with 23 goals in the regular season, and the best-of-five series against the Canadiens and Rangers went the distance. Marty Barry scored two goals, including the Cup-winner, in the 3-0 victory over New York.

■ **1943:** The Wings knocked the Maple Leafs out of the semifinals in six games, then swept the Bruins in four. Johnny Mowers blanked the Bruins in the final two games, 4-0 and 2-0, and Joe Carveth scored the Cup-winner, the last of his six goals in the playoffs.

■ **1950:** Gordie Howe suffered a near-fatal head injury in the first game against Toronto. In the finals against the Rangers, five games were played at Olympia Stadium and two at Toronto because a circus was booked at Madison Square Garden. Pete Babando scored the Cup-winning goal on a 15-foot backhander in the second overtime at Olympia for a 4-3 Wings victory. It was the first time Game 7 had gone into overtime.

■ **1952:** Goalie Terry Sawchuk, who won the Vezina Trophy with 12 shutouts and a 1.94 goals-against average, shut out Toronto twice in the first round and the Canadiens twice in the finals as the Wings won eight straight for the first double-sweep in Cup history. They finished with two straight 3-0 victories. The series marked the introduction of the octopus-throwing tradition — its eight tentacles symbolized the eight victories needed to win the Cup.

■ **1954:** The Wings polished off the Leafs in five games in the semifinals, then needed seven to beat Montreal. Tony Leswick's overtime goal at 4:29 gave Detroit the title in a 2-1 victory.

■ **1955:** After winning their seventh straight regular-season title, the Wings repeated as Stanley Cup champs for the first time in nearly 20 years. In the finals they played Montreal, missing suspended star Maurice (Rocket) Richard. Howe scored the Cup-winning goal in the seventh game, a 3-1 victory.